A RADIANT MASTERPIECE IN EXPLANATION OF THE POEM OF IBN ABEE DAAWUD:

AL-HAA'IYAH

SHAYKH ABDUR RAZZAAQ BIN ABDUL MUHSIN AL BADR

ISBN: 978-1-6344-3852-0

First Edition: Shawwâl 1435 A.H. / August 2014 C.E.

Cover Design: Aboo Sulaymaan Muhammad Abdul-Azim bin Joshua Baker

Translation by Raha ibn Donald Batts

Revision of Translation by Rasheed Ibn Estes Barbee

Editing: www.deliberateink.com

Typesetting and Formatting: Aboo Sulaymaan Muhammad Abdul-Azim bin Joshua Baker

Printing: Mega Printing

Subject: Tawheed/Minhaj/Aqeedah

Website: www.maktabatulirshad.com
E-mail: info@maktabatulirshad.com

فهرس

TABLE OF CONTENTS

ARABIC TEXT (AL-HAA'IYAH)

(1) تَمَسَّكْ بحَبْلِ اللهِ واتَّبِع الهُدَى ولا تَكُ بِدْعِيًّاً لَعلَّكَ تُفْلِحُ

(2) وَدِنْ بِكِتَابِ اللهِ والسُّنَنِ التِي أَتَتْ عَن رَسُولِ اللهِ تَنْجُ وَتَرْبَحُ

(3) وَقُلْ غَيْرُ مَخْلِوقٍ كَلامُ مَليكِنا بِذَلكَ دَانَ الأتْقِياءُ وأَفْصحُوا

(4) وَلا تَكُ فِي القُرْآنِ بالوَقْفِ قَائِلاً كَمَا قَالَ أَتْبَاعٌ لِجَهْمٍ وَأَسْجَحُواج

(5) ولا تَقُلِ القُرآنُ خَلقاً قرأتَهُ فإنَّ كَلامَ اللهِ باللفْظِ يُوضَحُ

(6) وَقُلْ يَتَجلَّى اللهُ للخَلْقِ جَهْرةً كَمَا البدْرُ لا يَخْفى وَرَبُّكَ أَوْضَحُ

(7) وَلَيْسَ بمْولُودٍ وليسَ بِوَالِدٍ وَلَيسَ لهُ شِبْهٌ تَعَالَى المسَبَّحُ

(8) وَقَدْ يُنكِرُ الجَهْميُّ هَذَا وعِنْدَنَا بِمِصْدَاقِ ما قُلْنَا حَدِيثٌ مُصَرِّحُ

(9) رَوَاهُ جَرِيرٌ عن مَقَالِ مُحَمَّدٍ فقُلْ مِثْلَ ما قَدْ قَالَ في ذَاكَ تَنْجَحُ

(10) وَقَدْ يُنكِرُ الجَهْمِيُّ أَيضًا يَمِينَهُ   وَكِلْتَا يَدَيْهِ بالفواضِلِ تَنْفَحُ

(11) وَقُلْ يَنْزِلُ الجَبَّارُ فِي كُلِّ لَيْلَةٍ   بِلا كَيْفَ جَلَّ الواحدُ المتَمَدِّحُ

(12) إلى طَبَقِ الدُّنيا يَمُنُّ بِفَضْلِهِ   فَتُفْرَجُ أَبْوابُ السَّماءِ وتُفْتَحُ

(13) يَقولُ : ألا مُسْتغفِرٌ يَلْقَ غَافِرًا   ومُسْتَمنِحٌ خَيْرًا ورِزقًا فأَمْنَحُ

(14) رَوَى ذَاكَ قَومٌ لا يُرَدُّ حَدِيثَهم   ألا خَابَ قَوْمٌ كذَّبُوهُم وقُبِّحوا

(15) وَقُلْ إنَّ خَيْرَ النَّاسِ بَعْدَ مُحَمَّدٍ   وَزِيرَاهُ قُدْمًا ثُمَّ عُثْمَانُ أَرْجَحُ

(16) وَرابِعُهُم خَيْرُ البرِيَّةِ بَعْدَهُم   عَلِيٌّ حليفُ الخَيرِ بالخَيرِ مُنْجِحُ

(17) وإنَّهمُ و الرَّهْطُ لا رَيْبَ فِيهِمُ   عَلَى نُجُبِ الفِرْدَوْسِ في الخُلْدِ تَسْرَحُ

(18) سَعِيدٌ وسَعْدٌ وابنُ عَوْفٍ وطَلْحَةٌ   وعَامِرُ فِهْرٍ والزُّبَيْرُ المُمَدَّحُ

(19) وَقُلْ خَيْرَ قولٍ في الصَّحابةِ كُلِّهِمْ   ولا تَكُ طَعَّاناً تَعِيبُ وَتَجْرَحُ

(20) فَقَدْ نَطَقَ الوَحْيُ المُبينُ بِفَضْلِهِـــمْ وفي الفَتْحِ آيٌ في الصَّحابةِ تَمْدَحُ

(21) وبِالقَـدَرِ المقْـدُورِ أيْقِنْ فإنَّهُ دِعَامَةُ عقْدِ الدِّينِ والدِّينُ أفْيَـحُ

(22) وَلا تُنْكِرَنْ جهلاً نَكِيرًا ومُنْكَـراً وَلا الحَوضَ والمِيزانَ إنَّـكَ تُنْصَـحُ

(23) وقُـلْ يُخْرِجُ اللهُ العَظيمُ بِفَضلِـهِ مِن النارِ أجْسادًا مِن الفَحْمِ تُطْرَحُ

(24) عَلَى النَّهرِ في الفِردوسِ تَحْيا بِمائِهِ كَحَبِّ حَميلِ السَّيْلِ إذْ جاءَ يَطْفَـحُ

(25) فإنَّ رَسُـولَ اللـهِ للخَلـقِ شَافـعٌ وقُلْ فِي عَذابِ القَبرِ حـقٌّ مُوَضَّحُ

(26) ولا تُكْفِّرَنَّ أهْلَ الصَّلاةِ وإنْ عَصَـوا فكلُّهُمْ يَعْصِي وذُو العَرشِ يَصْفَـحُ

(27) ولا تَعتقِـــدْ رَأيَ الخَــوارجِ إنَّـــهُ مَقَالٌ لِمَنْ يهـواهُ يُرْدِي ويَفْضَحُ

(28) ولا تَـكُ مُرْجِيًّا لَعُوبًا بِدِينِـهِ ألا إنَّـــما المُرْجـــيُّ بالـــدِّينِ يَمْـــزَحُ

(29) وقُـلْ إنَّما الإيمانُ قَـوْلٌ ونيَّـةٌ وفِعْلٌ عَلَى قَـولِ النبيِّ مُصَرَّحُ

(30) وينْقُصُ طَـوْرًا بالمعَاصِي وَتَـارةً بطَاعَتِهِ يَنْمِي وفي الوَزنِ يَرْجَحُ

(31) وَدَعْ عنكَ آراءَ الرِّجالِ وَقـولَهُـم فَقَوْلُ رَسُولِ اللهِ أَزكى وَأَشْـرَحُ

(32) وَلا تَكُ مِـن قـوْمٍ تَلَهَّـوْ بِدِينِهِـم فَتَطْعـنَ في أَهَلِ الحَدَيثِ وتَقْـدَحُ

(33) إذا مَا اعتقـدْتَ الدَّهْرَ يا صَاحِ هذِه فَأَنْـتَ عَلـى خَيْـرٍ تَبيتُ وتُصْبِحُ

BRIEF BIOGRAPHY OF THE EXPLAINER

His name: Shaykh 'Abdur-Razzaaq Bin 'Abdil-Muhsin Al-'Abbad Al-Badr.

He is the son of Al-'Allamah Muhaddith of Medina Shaykh 'Abdul-Muhsin Al-'Abbad Al-Badr.

Birth: He was born on the 22nd day of Dhul-Qaddah in the year 1382 AH in az-Zal'fi, Kingdom of Saudia Arabia. He currently resides in Al-Medina Al-Munawwarah.

Current occupation: He is a member of the teaching staff at the Islamic University, in Al-Medina.

Scholastic certifications: Doctorate in Aqeedah.

The Shaykh has authored books, researches, as well as numerous explanations in different sciences. Among them:

1. Fiqh of Supplications & Ad-Dhkaar.
2. Hajj & refinement of Souls,
3. Explanation of the book "Exemplary Principles" By Shaykh Uthaymeen P (May Allâh have mercy upon him).

4. Explanation of the book “the principles of Names & Attributes” authored by Shaykh-ul-Islam Ibnul-Qayyim (May Allâh have mercy upon him).

5. Explanation of the book “Good Words” authored by Shaykh-ul-Islam Ibn Qayyim (May Allâh have mercy upon him).

6. Explanation of the book “Aqeedah Tahaawiyyah”.

7. Explanation of the book “Fusuul: Biography of the Messenger) By Ibn Katheer (May Allâh have mercy upon him).

8. He has a full explanation of the book “Aadaab-ul-Muf’rad” authored by Imam Bukhari (May Allâh have mercy upon him).

From the most distinguished scholars whom he has taken knowledge and acquired knowledge from are:

1. His father Al-‘Allamah Shaykh ‘Abdul-Muhsin Al-Badr—may Allâh preserve him.

2. Al-‘Allamah Shaykh Ibn Baaz—may Allâh have mercy upon him.

3. Al-‘Allamah Shaykh Muhammad Bin Saleh Al-‘Uthaymeen—may Allâh have mercy upon him.

4. Shaykh Ali Nasir Faqeehi—may Allâh preserve him.

INTRODUCTION

All the praise is for Allaah, the Lord of all that exists. The good end is for those who have Taqwaa. May prayers and peace be upon the Imaam of the Messengers; our Prophet Muhammad, his family members, and his companions, all together. As to proceed:

This is a summarized explanation of the brilliant couplet; the radiant poem known as Al-Haa'iyah الحائية by its author, the Imaam, the verifier, the precise preserver, the Shaykh of Baghdad, Aboo Bakr 'Abdullaah ibn Aboo Daawud Sulaymaan ibn Al-Ash'ath As-Sijistaanee; the son of the author of the Sunan, the well-known Imaam, may Allaah have mercy upon the both of them.

It is a poem, the mention of which, is widespread and has a lofty status; it is eloquent in its wording and easy to memorize. It has a lofty status and a high position with the people of knowledge of old and later times. Its transmission from Ibn Abee Daawud, may Allaah have mercy upon him, has been successively narrated. A number of the people of knowledge have narrated it from him; such as Al-Aajuree, Ibn Battah, Ibn Saaheen, and others. The three of them are from the students of the Shaykh. A number of the people of knowledge have endeavored to explain it.

Adh-Dhahabee, may Allaah have mercy upon him, said when speaking about this poem and clarifying its importance: *"This poem has been successively narrated from its author. Al-Aajuree reported it and compiled an explanation of it as did Aboo Abdullaah Ibn Battah within Al-Ibaanah."*[1] From those who explained it was Ibn Al-Banaa.[2] As for their explanations, I do not know them to be in existence (any longer).[3] From those who explained it was Imaam As-Safaareenee. His explanation of it is printed in two volumes under the title: Lawaa'ih Al-Anwaar As-Saniyah wa Lawaaqih Al-Afkaar As-Sunniyah Sharh Qaseedah Ibn Abee Daawud Al-Haa'iyah Fee 'Aqeedah Ahlil-Aathaar As-Salafiyyah; with the checking of the noble brother, Shaykh 'Abdullaah Al-Busayree, may Allaah preserve him. I have entitled this explanation:

التحفة السنية شرح منظومة ابن أبي داود الحائية

---

[1] Al-'Uloo 2/1223

[2] Ibn Rajab mentioned that within the appendix of Tabaqaat Al-Hanaabilah 1/35

[3] A short while ago I came across the explanation of Ibn Al-Banna for Al-Haa'iyah handwritten within the library of Adh-Dhaahiriyah in Damascus.

"The Radiant Masterpiece in Explanation of the Poem of Ibn Abee Daawud: Al-Haa'iyah."

Its origin is lessons which I gave in the Masjid of the Islamic University in the Prophetic City in the year 1417 H. One of the students of knowledge transcribed it for me—and he is the noble brother Yahyaa ibn 'Alee ibn Yahyaa; then I reviewed it, added to it, and revised it as much as I was able. It is a small effort and a modest and humble presentation. So that which it contains from truth and correctness, then it is from Allaah Alone, and that which it contains from error and shortcoming, then it is due to my weakness, shortcomings, and scantiness of knowledge.

I must also thank all who contributed any type of assistance and cooperation in publishing this book, whether that be in arranging it and typesetting or review and editing it or printing and publishing it. I ask Allaah to reward all parties with the best reward. Similarly, I ask Allaah to bring benefit by way of it and to accept it with a goodly acceptance and to make it sincerely for the sake of seeking His Noble Face and to make it a benefit for His slaves; indeed he is the All-Hearing, the Responsive.

May prayers and peace be upon our Prophet Muhammad, his family, and companions.

BRIEF BIOGRAPHY OF THE POET IBN ABEE DAAWUD

His name, his lineage and his Kunyah:

He is the Imaam, the ‘Allaamah, the Haafidh, the Shaykh of Baghdad; ‘Abdullaah the son of Imaam Aboo Daawud Sulaymaan ibn Al-Ash’ath, Aboo Bakr As-Sijistaanee.

His Birth:

The Imaam Aboo Bakr Ibn Aboo Daawud was born in Sijistaan in the year 230 H.

His Upbringing and Seeking of Knowledge:

His father traveled with him throughout the east and the west when he was a child to Khurasaan and Asbahaan, Baghdad, Al-Koofah, Makkah, Madeenah, Shaam, Egypt, and other places, listening and writing; and he took residence in Bagdad. The first Shaykh, who he learned from, was Muhammad Ibn Aslam At-Toosee, and his father was very pleased with that due to the nobility of Muhammad Ibn Aslam. He was one who had the utmost seriousness ever since his childhood in acquiring and seeking knowledge. From the signs of this seriousness was his statement, may Allaah have mercy upon him: *"I entered Koofah having only one Dirham with me, and I purchased with it 30 Mudd of fava beans and I would eat from it and write (Hadeeths) from Aboo Sa'eed Al-Ashaj. The fava beans had not depleted until I had written thirty-thousand narrations. Between that which was Maqtoo' (disconnected) and Mursal (narrations which exclude mention of the companion)."*[4]

He was precise memorizer. He, may Allaah have mercy upon him said: *"I narrated from my memory thirty-six-thousand Hadeeths in Asbahaan and I was uncertain regarding seven Hadeeths from amongst them. So when I had departed, I found within my book that five of them were exactly as I had narrated them."*[5]

His student, Aboo Hafs ibn Shaaheen said in clarification of the strength of his memory: *"Ibn Aboo Daawud dictated to us for a number of years, and I never saw him write with his hand, he only would dictate from his memory. He would sit upon the Minbar after he had become old and his son, Aboo Ma'mar, would sit on the step beneath him holding a book and he would say: 'Hadeeth such and such and he (Ibn*

[4] Refer to Taareekh Bagdad 9/466-467.

[5] Refer to Taareekh Bagdad 9/466.

Aboo Daawud) would recite it from his memory until a gathering would come.'"

Some of his Teachers:

He narrated from his father as well as Ahmad ibn Saalih, Muhammad ibn Bashaar, 'Amr Ibn 'Uthmaan Al-Himsee, Is'haaq Al-Kawsij, 'Amr ibn 'Alee Al-Fallaas and Muhammad ibn Yahyaa Adh-Dhuhalee.

Some of his Students:

A large number of people narrated from him, from them was Ibn Hibbaan, the author of As-Saheeh as well as Abul-Hasan Ad-Daaraqutnee and Aboo Hafs ibn Shaaheen and Aboo Ahmad Al-Haakim, as well as Ibn Battah and Muhammad ibn 'Umar ibn Zanboor Al-Warraaq, as well as Aboo Muslim Muhammad Ibn Ahmad Al-Kaatib, and 'Eesaa ibn 'Alee Al-Wazeer, and Aboo Qaasim ibn Hibaabah.

His status in knowledge and the praise of the scholars for him:

Al-Haafidh Aboo Muhammad Al-Kallaal said: *"Ibn Aboo Daawud was the Imaam of the people of Iraq and the Sultan had given him authority over the Minbar. During his time in Iraq, the chains of narrations were attributed to him, and none reached that which he did from precision and acuteness."*

Al-Khateeb Al-Baghdaadee said concerning him: *"He was a Faqeeh, a scholar, and a memorizer."*[6]

Ibn Khalkaan said concerning him: *"Aboo Bakr Ibn Aboo Daawud was from the major memorizers in Baghdad. He was a scholar, one who had Fiqh and an Imaam."*

Adh-Dhahabee said: *"He was from the oceans of knowledge to the point that some of the scholars gave him precedence over his father (in knowledge)."*

Adh-Dhahabee also said: *"Aboo Bakr was from the preeminent memorizers from the generations beneath his father. He compiled a number of writings and was from the heads of the Hanaabilah in Bagdad."*

He also said: *"The man is from the major scholars of the Muslims and from the most eminent memorizers."*

His Creed:

He, may Allaah have mercy upon him, was upon the Aqeedah of the Salaf; the people of Hadeeth; and there is nothing that proves this more than his poem, Al-Haa'iyah. Within it—although it is concise—he affirms the general creed upon the path of Ahlus-Sunnah Wal-Jamaa'ah. It is affirmed by him that he said,

[6] Refer to Tareekh Bagdad 9/464.

commenting upon this poem: *"This is my statement and the statement of my father; and the statement of our scholars and likewise the statement of the scholars from those who we have not seen as has been conveyed to us from them. So he who says upon me other than this then he has lied."*

It is a magnificent poem in affirmation of the correct creed which Ahlus-Sunnah Wal-Jamaa'ah are upon indicating the great and eminent status of its author and the excellence of his creed and the beautiful nature of his advice.

At any rate, the leadership of its author and his status is known amongst the people of knowledge. He is from the Imaams of the Salaf and the preeminent men of the Sunnah, and the memorizers of Hadeeth and the callers to the truth and guidance and his leadership and virtue is agreed upon.

His Writings:

Adh-Dhahabee has described him as being a man of authorship; from those works are the following:

As-Sunan, Al-Ba'ath, Al-Masaahif, Shari'atul Maqari', and An-Naasikh wal-Mansookh.

His death:

He, may Allaah have mercy upon him, died in Bagdad in the month of Dhul-Hijjah in the year three-sixteen after the Hijrah while being eighty-seven years old, and it was said that three-thousand people or more prayed over him. He left behind three sons whose names were;

1. Abdul-A'laa
2. Muhammad
3. Aboo Ma'mar 'Ubaydullaah

And he left behind five daughters; may Allaah have mercy upon him and forgive him as well as all of the Imaams of the Muslims.

CLINGING TO THE BOOK AND THE SUNNAH AND AVOIDING INNOVATIONS

(1) تَمَسَّكْ بِحَبْلِ اللهِ واتَّبِع الهُدَى ولا تَكُ بِدْعِيّاً لَعلَّكَ تُفْلِحُ

(2) وَدِنْ بِكِتَابِ اللهِ والسُّنَنِ التِي أَتَتْ عَن رَسُولِ اللهِ تَنْجُ وَتَرْبَحُ

1. *Hold tightly to the Rope of Allaah and the guidance,*

And do not be an innovator, and thus you may be successful.

2. *And practice your religion based on the Book of Allaah and the Sunan which*

Have come from the Messenger of Allaah, so you will be saved and gain profit.

Explanation

The poet began his poem regarding the creed with these two magnificent stanzas. And these lines of poetry contain the call to cling to the Book and the Sunnah, and to beware of innovations. He has begun with them before clarifying the creed and its affairs in accordance with the path of Ahlus-Sunnah within the books of creed since their way, in most instances, was to begin with this affair; and this was an example of them of denoting the source of derivation for the Usool of the religion and its subsidiary branches in order that the structure of the creed and its basis be upon a sound foundation and strong correct principles. When the servant makes the source from which he derives his creed and the source upon which the principles are predicated to be the Book and the Sunnah, then he will see that which is besides it from sources to be rubbish and he will not take anything from them nor will he make them be a source for him in his religion and his creed. He will only take from the pure source, and the pure spring which is neither soiled nor defiled; and thus by way of this his creed will be safe, and his Eemaan will be sound.

The source of Ahlus-Sunnah in derivation is the Book and the Sunnah. They take from them, derive their evidence from them, and rely on them. They do not deviate from them in the least. Rather, they are as Al-Awzaa'ee said:

> "We go with the Book and the Sunnah wherever they go."

They do not invent anything from themselves. Shaykh Al-Islaam, may Allaah have mercy upon him, stated:

> "The creed does not belong to me nor to anyone greater than myself. The creed belongs to Allaah and His Messenger (ﷺ)."

So from Allaah is the Message and upon the Messenger is the conveyance of the Message and upon us is belief and submission. Due to this, we find the books of Ahlus-Sunnah beginning with mention of the source before explaining the creed. This is that which we derive from that which the Messenger of Allaah (ﷺ) would constantly do within the Friday sermon. He would always say at the beginning of it:

أَمَّا بَعْدُ ؛ فَإِنَّ أَصْدَقَ الْحَدِيثِ كِتَابُ اللهِ وَ خَيْرَ الْهَدِي هَدِي مُحَمَّدٍ - صَلَّى اللهُ عَلَيْهِ وَ سَلَّمَ وَ شَرَّ الْأُمُورِ مُحْدَثَاتُهَا

"As to proceed; indeed the truest speech is the Book of Allaah the best guidance is the guidance of Muhammad (صَلَّى ٱللَّهُ عَلَيْهِ وَسَلَّمَ) and the worst of all matters and the newly invented matters."[7]

And his (صَلَّى ٱللَّهُ عَلَيْهِ وَسَلَّمَ), repetition of that every Friday contains emphasis for the importance of giving due consideration to this source and the necessity of preserving and safeguarding it.

Concerning his statement: تَمسَّكْ *"Cling"* Clinging in the language means: To hold fast to something and be steadfast upon it. This is derived from the statement of Allaah the Exalted:

﴿ وَٱعْتَصِمُوا۟ بِحَبْلِ ٱللَّهِ جَمِيعًا وَلَا تَفَرَّقُوا۟ ۚ وَٱذْكُرُوا۟ نِعْمَتَ ٱللَّهِ عَلَيْكُمْ إِذْ كُنتُمْ أَعْدَآءً فَأَلَّفَ بَيْنَ قُلُوبِكُمْ فَأَصْبَحْتُم بِنِعْمَتِهِۦٓ إِخْوَٰنًا وَكُنتُمْ عَلَىٰ شَفَا حُفْرَةٍ مِّنَ ٱلنَّارِ فَأَنقَذَكُم مِّنْهَا ۗ كَذَٰلِكَ يُبَيِّنُ ٱللَّهُ لَكُمْ ءَايَٰتِهِۦ لَعَلَّكُمْ تَهْتَدُونَ ﴿١٠٣﴾ ﴾

And hold fast, all of you together, to the Rope of Allaah and be not divided among yourselves, and remember Allaah's Favor on you, for you were enemies one to another but He joined

[7] Reported by Muslim no. 8607 from the Hadeeth of Jaabir Ibn 'Abdullah, may Allaah be pleased with him.

your hearts together, so that, by His Grace, you became brethren, and you were on the brink of a pit of Fire, and He saved you from it. Thus Allaah makes His Ayât (proofs, evidence, verses, lessons, signs, revelations, etc.,) clear to you, that you may be guided. [8]

Likewise the statement of Allaah, the Exalted:

﴿ وَٱلَّذِينَ يُمَسِّكُونَ بِٱلْكِتَٰبِ وَأَقَامُوا۟ ٱلصَّلَوٰةَ إِنَّا لَا نُضِيعُ أَجْرَ ٱلْمُصْلِحِينَ ﴿١٧٠﴾ ﴾

And as to those who hold fast to the Book and perform the prayer; certainly, We shall never waste the reward of those who do righteous deeds. [9]

Concerning the *"...Rope of Allaah"* the scholars have several statements concerning its meaning. The majority of them, according to the scholars of Tafseer, say that it means: the Qur'aan; as has been mentioned by Ibn Al-Qayyim, may Allaah have mercy upon him. And it is that which is intended by the poet here because he mentions the Sunnah thereafter.

---

[8] Soorah Aali Imran (3:103)

[9] Soorah Al-A'raf (7:170)

The poet, may Allaah have mercy upon him, within his statement: *"Hold tightly to the Rope of Allaah,"* is addressing the Sunnee and saying to him: Let your point of reference always and eternally be the Book of Allaah and along with your clinging to it: *"Follow the guidance"* meaning: the Sunnah. The term guidance within the Book and the Sunnah are applied to two affairs:

- The first is At-Tawfeeq and inspiration.
- The second is indicating clarification and directing

By way of the context, it is possible to know that which is intended. So the statement of Allaah the Exalted:

﴿ إِنَّكَ لَا تَهْدِى مَنْ أَحْبَبْتَ وَلَٰكِنَّ ٱللَّهَ يَهْدِى مَن يَشَآءُ ۚ وَهُوَ أَعْلَمُ بِٱلْمُهْتَدِينَ ﴿٥٦﴾ ﴾

Verily! You (O Muhammad ﷺ) guide not whom you like, but Allaah guides whom He wills. And He knows best those who are the guided. [10]

Likewise, the statement of Allaah the Exalted:

---

[10] Soorah Al-Qasas (28:56)

﴿ ۞ لَّيْسَ عَلَيْكَ هُدَىٰهُمْ وَلَٰكِنَّ ٱللَّهَ يَهْدِى مَن يَشَآءُ ﴾

Not upon you (Muhammad ﷺ) is their guidance, but Allaah guides whom He wills. [11]

Likewise, the statement of Allaah the Exalted:

﴿ مَن يَهْدِ ٱللَّهُ فَهُوَ ٱلْمُهْتَدِى ۖ وَمَن يُضْلِلْ فَأُو۟لَٰٓئِكَ هُمُ ٱلْخَٰسِرُونَ ﴿١٧٨﴾ ﴾

Whomsoever Allaah guides, he is the guided one, and whomsoever He sends astray, those! They are the losers. [12]

As well as the statement of Allaah the Exalted:

﴿ ٱهْدِنَا ٱلصِّرَٰطَ ٱلْمُسْتَقِيمَ ﴿٦﴾ ﴾

Guide us to the Straight Way. [13]

All of these verses speak of the guidance of At-Tawfeeq, and this is not for anyone except Allaah the Exalted. The Prophet (ﷺ) would seek the guidance of his Lord within his supplication, and he would say:

اللَّهُمَّ إِنِّي أَسْأَلُكَ الْهُدَى وَ السَّدَادَ

[11] Soorah Al-Baqarah (2:272)
[12] Soorah Al-A'raf (7:178)
[13] Soorah Al-Fatihah (1:6)

"O Allaah, I ask You for guidance and uprightness."[14]

So the One who opens the chests and gives Tawfeeq and guidance is Allaah. Due to this, Allaah, the Exalted said, addressing His Prophet (ﷺ):

﴿ إِنَّكَ لَا تَهْدِي مَنْ أَحْبَبْتَ وَلَٰكِنَّ اللَّهَ يَهْدِي مَن يَشَاءُ ۚ وَهُوَ أَعْلَمُ بِالْمُهْتَدِينَ ﴿٥٦﴾ ﴾

Verily! You (O Muhammad ﷺ) guide not whom you like, but Allaah guides whom He wills. And He knows best those who are the guided. [15]

And the other guidance is the guidance of directing and clarification. Allaah, the Exalted has said:

﴿ وَأَمَّا ثَمُودُ فَهَدَيْنَاهُمْ فَاسْتَحَبُّوا الْعَمَىٰ عَلَى الْهُدَىٰ فَأَخَذَتْهُمْ صَاعِقَةُ الْعَذَابِ الْهُونِ بِمَا كَانُوا يَكْسِبُونَ ﴿١٧﴾ ﴾

And as for Thamûd, We showed and made clear to them the Path of Truth through Our

[14] Reported by Muslim no. 2725 from the Hadeeth of 'Alee Ibn Abee Taalib, may Allaah have mercy upon him.
[15] Soorah Al-Qasas (28:56)

> **Messenger, but they preferred blindness to guidance, so the Sâ'iqah (a destructive awful cry) of disgracing torment seized them, because of what they used to earn.** [16]

Had this been in reference to the guidance of Tawfeeq, then they would not have preferred blindness over guidance. Likewise Allaah, the Exalted has said:

﴿ وَهَدَيْنَٰهُ ٱلنَّجْدَيْنِ ﴿١٠﴾ ﴾

> **And shown him the two ways (good and evil)?** [17]

This guidance is for the prophets, the righteous and the scholars. From that is the statement of Allaah in reference to His Prophet (ﷺ):

> **And verily, you (O Muhammad ﷺ) are indeed guiding (mankind) to the Straight Path.** [18]

Likewise the statement of Allaah, the Exalted:

---

[16] Soorah Fussilat (41:17)

[17] Soorah Al-Balad (90:10)

[18] Soorah Ash-Shura (42:52)

﴿ وَجَعَلْنَا مِنْهُمْ أَئِمَّةً يَهْدُونَ بِأَمْرِنَا لَمَّا صَبَرُوا ۖ وَكَانُوا بِآيَاتِنَا يُوقِنُونَ ﴿٢٤﴾ ﴾

And We made from among them (Children of Israel), leaders, giving guidance under Our Command when they were patient and used to believe with certainty in Our Ayât. [19]

The statement of the poet when he said: *"And follow the guidance."* Means: follow the path of guidance and uprightness which the Messenger of Allaah (ﷺ) has clarified and guided to. It is the best guidance and the most complete of it. Within the statement of the Prophet (ﷺ) he said:

وَ خَيْرُ الْهُدَى هُدَى مُحَمَّدٍ

"The best guidance is the guidance of Muhammad."

In another narration he said:

وَ خَيْرُ الْهَدِي

"The best path..."

[19] Soorah As-Sajdah (32:24)

الهُدى *Al-Hudaa* refers to directing and guiding. الهدي *Al-Hady* is the path, and his path (ﷺ) is that which he clarified to the people and guided them towards from that which his Lord had revealed to him; and he did not speak of his own desire. It was only a revelation revealed to him. His guidance is the best provision for the Day of Return and the standing before the Lord of the servants. So within the poet's encouragement, may Allaah have mercy upon him, towards clinging to the Book and the Sunnah there lies a refutation of the statement of the deviant group known as the Qur'aanites; those who say we do not take except the Qur'aan. Those who are like this, then they do not even take the Qur'aan; because Allaah has commanded within His Book, in numerous verses, to take to the Sunnah and hold fast to it. Due to this, the servant cannot be one who clings to the Qur'aan except when he takes from the Sunnah. So it is a must that one takes to the two affairs together.

Allaah, the Exalted has commanded the Mothers of the Believers within His statement:

﴿ وَاذْكُرْنَ مَا يُتْلَىٰ فِي بُيُوتِكُنَّ مِنْ آيَاتِ اللَّهِ وَالْحِكْمَةِ ۚ إِنَّ اللَّهَ كَانَ لَطِيفًا خَبِيرًا ﴿٣٤﴾ ﴾

And remember (O you the members of the Prophet's family, the Graces of your Lord), that which is recited in your houses of the Verses of Allaah and Al-Hikmah (i.e. Prophet's Sunnah legal ways). Verily, Allaah is Ever Most Courteous, Well Acquainted with all things. [20]

And likewise Allaah, the Glorified has said:

﴿وَمَآ ءَاتَىٰكُمُ ٱلرَّسُولُ فَخُذُوهُ وَمَا نَهَىٰكُمْ عَنْهُ فَٱنتَهُوا۟ۚ﴾

And whatsoever the Messenger (Muhammad ﷺ) gives you, take it, and whatsoever he forbids you, abstain (from it). [21]

The first half of the first line of poetry, which is his statement:

"Hold fast to the rope of Allaah and follow the guidance,"

contains demarcation of the source of derivation. And once he had demarcated it, he warned against opposing it; wherein he said:

"And do not be an innovator."

---

[20] Soorah Al-Ahzab (33:34)

[21] Soorah Al-Hashr (59:7)

By way of this context, he is indicating an important principle. It is that he who diverges from the rope of Allaah and from the Sunnah, then he has taken to the path of innovation and misguidance. Due to this, the people of knowledge have defined Bid'ah as being that which is not the Sunnah. The poet, may Allaah have mercy upon him, is saying:

Do not be an innovator by way of abandoning the Book and the Sunnah.

By way of this he is indicating the deep abyss which all of the innovators have fallen into, and it is the abandonment of the Book and the Sunnah. Otherwise, they would have been from Ahlus-Sunnah wal-Jamaa'ah, and they would not have been from the people of desires and innovations. Therefore, the innovator is he who abandons the Book and the Sunnah and does not cling to them nor does he derive his religion from them. He who investigates the general populous of the people of innovations will find that the source of their deviation lies in abandonment of clinging to the Book and the Sunnah; either in creed by way of taking to the intellects and opinions or dreams, or false reports or other than this from that which the people of desires have taken a source of derivation for themselves.

His statement: *"...perhaps you will be successful,"* this is the result of clinging to the Book and the Sunnah and avoiding innovations. Al-Falaah is a comprehensive term for all good within the Dunyaa and the Hereafter. It is said that there is no word in the language that is more comprehensive of all good than the word Falaah. And Al-Falaah cannot be except by way of clinging to the Book and the Sunnah and staying far away from innovations. He who does not cling to the Book and the Sunnah and he takes anything from those false forms of reference, and then he will not be successful. Due to this, there has come on the authority of Imaam Ahmad, may Allaah have mercy upon him, that he said:

> "No one has even embarked upon theological rhetoric and been successful."

When Ash-Shaafi'ee debated with Bishr and had conquered him, Bishr exited, and Ash-Shaafi'ee said:

"He will never be successful."

And this is the meaning which the noble Qur'aan indicates as is at the beginning of Soorah Al-Baqarah wherein Allaah, the Exalted has said:

﴿ الٓمٓ ﴿١﴾ ذَٰلِكَ ٱلۡكِتَٰبُ لَا رَيۡبَۛ فِيهِۛ هُدٗى لِّلۡمُتَّقِينَ ﴿٢﴾ ٱلَّذِينَ يُؤۡمِنُونَ بِٱلۡغَيۡبِ وَيُقِيمُونَ ٱلصَّلَوٰةَ وَمِمَّا
رَزَقۡنَٰهُمۡ يُنفِقُونَ ﴿٣﴾ وَٱلَّذِينَ يُؤۡمِنُونَ بِمَآ أُنزِلَ إِلَيۡكَ وَمَآ أُنزِلَ مِن قَبۡلِكَ وَبِٱلۡأٓخِرَةِ هُمۡ يُوقِنُونَ ﴿٤﴾
أُوْلَٰٓئِكَ عَلَىٰ هُدٗى مِّن رَّبِّهِمۡۖ وَأُوْلَٰٓئِكَ هُمُ ٱلۡمُفۡلِحُونَ ﴿٥﴾ ﴾

Alif-Lâm-Mîm. This is the Book (the Qur'aan), whereof there is no doubt, a guidance to those who are pious. Who believe in the Unseen and establish the prayer, and spend out of what we have provided for them. And who believe in (the Qur'aan and the Sunnah) which has been sent down (revealed) to you (Muhammad--peace be upon him) and in that which was sent down before you and they believe with certainty in the Hereafter. They are on (true) guidance from their Lord, and they are successful. [22]

The statement of the poet when he said: *"Perhaps..."* here this does not denote something which is hoped for, because he who clings to the Book and the Sunnah, then his success has been actualized unless it is intended by way of the action of the servant and his actualization of this affair and perfection of it; the clinging to the Book and the Sunnah.

---

22 Soorah Al-Baqarah (2:1-5)

Then the poet, may Allaah have mercy upon him, emphasizes clinging to the Book and the Sunnah by way of his statement:

> *And practice your religion based on the Book of Allaah and the Sunan which*
>
> *Have come from the Messenger of Allaah, so you will be saved and gain profit.*

His statement: دِنْ (Practice your religion) This is a command derived from the verb دان يدين ديناً The meaning of it is: Establish your religion upon the Book and the Sunnah and believe and obey and adhere to that which has come to them by way of affirmation of the reports and enacting the commands and abandoning the prohibitions. His statement:

"And the Sunan, which have come from the Messenger of Allaah."

Sunan is the plural of Sunnah. What is intended is the Ahaadeeth, which have been reported from the Messenger of Allaah (ﷺ) and have been affirmed by him.

So his statement: *"...that have come from the Messenger of Allaah."* contains a restriction and guidance towards the fact that the Sunan must be authentically reported so that they may be taken and accepted. If they are authentically reported, whether they are by way of *At-Tawaatur* (consecutively narrated reports) or *Al-Ahad* (singular narrations) then they constitute evidence and they are a basis in all of the affairs of the religion; in creed and other than it.

His statement: *"...you will be saved,"* he did not mention from what. This is in order that the salvation would be general from every type of evil and calamity in the Dunyaa and the Hereafter.

His statement: *"...and you will gain profit,"* this is an increase in the safety. So safety is the choicest of all wealth and above it there are various types of profit in accordance with the strength of the individual's holding fast to the Book and the Sunnah. He shall have profit in the world as well as the Hereafter.

Allaah, the Exalted has said:

﴿ قُلْنَا ٱهْبِطُوا۟ مِنْهَا جَمِيعًا فَإِمَّا يَأْتِيَنَّكُم مِّنِّى هُدًى فَمَن تَبِعَ هُدَاىَ فَلَا خَوْفٌ عَلَيْهِمْ وَلَا هُمْ يَحْزَنُونَ ﴿٣٨﴾ ﴾

We said: "Get down all of you from this place (the Paradise), then whenever there comes to you Guidance from Me, and whoever follows

My Guidance, there shall be no fear on them, nor shall they grieve. [23]

Allaah, the Exalted has also said:

﴿ قَالَ ٱهْبِطَا مِنْهَا جَمِيعًۢا بَعْضُكُمْ لِبَعْضٍ عَدُوٌّ فَإِمَّا يَأْتِيَنَّكُم مِّنِّى هُدًى فَمَنِ ٱتَّبَعَ هُدَاىَ فَلَا يَضِلُّ وَلَا يَشْقَىٰ ﴿١٢٣﴾ ﴾

Then if there comes to you guidance from Me, then whoever follows My Guidance shall neither go astray nor fall into distress and misery. [24]

There has come on the authority of Ibn 'Abbas, may Allaah be pleased with him, that he said in this regard:

> "Allaah has made it binding upon Himself for the one who recites the Qur'aan and acts upon that which is within it that he will not go astray in the Dunyaa, and he will not be wretched in the hereafter."

---

[23] Soorah Al-Baqarah (2:38)

[24] Soorah Ta-Ha (20:123)

THE ATTRIBUTE OF SPEECH

(3) وَقُـلْ غَيْـرُ مَخْلوقٍ كَلامُ مَليكِنا   بِـذَلكَ دَانَ الأَتْقِياءُ وأَفْصحُـوا

(4) وَلا تَكُ فِي القُرْآنِ بالوَقْفِ   كَمَا قَالَ أَتْبَاعٌ لِجَهْمٍ وَأَسْجَحُواج
قَائِـلاً

(5) ولا تَقُـلِ القُرآنُ خَـلقاً قـرأتَـهُ   فإِنَّ كَـلامَ اللهِ باللفْظِ يُـوضَحُ

3. *And say: Not a created thing is the Speech of our great King,*

Such was the religion of the pious ones (before us) which they clearly expressed.

4. *And do not be a person who takes no position on the Qur'aan,*

As did the followers of Jahm, and they had been too lax (to take the right position).

5. *And do not say that the Qur'aan is created, as I have recited it,*

Since the Speech of Allaah, through its recitation, is made clear.

Explanation

Perhaps the poet began with this Attribute before mentioning other than it from Attributes due to it being appropriate to the context. This is because he began with the first two stanzas by mentioning clinging to the Book and the Sunnah. So when he mentioned the obligation of clinging to the Qur'aan, he began thereafter by mentioning lines of poetry regarding it. So he mentioned the creed of Ahlus-Sunnah as it relates to the Qur'aan and a refutation against those who oppose the truth and avoided it and rejected the creed of Ahlus-Sunnah regarding it. So these stanzas contain a concise clarification of the creed of Ahlus-Sunnah as it relates to this issue. As well as a refutation of various categories of the people of innovations and they are of numerous groups. The poet is indicating some of them; so he began, may Allaah have mercy upon him, by speaking regarding this issue with his statement:

"And say: Not a created thing is the Speech of our great King,"

So his statement: *"Say..."* is an address to the person of the Sunnah who clings to the Book and the Sunnah and it means: *Say, believing in it and having Eemaan in this affair, having no doubt in it nor being hesitant.* For when the word "statement" is used it implies the statement made with the heart and the tongue.

And from that is the statement of Allaah, the Exalted, wherein He said:

﴿ قُولُوٓاْ ءَامَنَّا بِٱللَّهِ ﴾

Say (O Muslims), "We believe in Allaah [25]

Meaning, say this with your heart having Eemaan and firm belief as well as with your tongues pronouncing it and articulating it. The statement of the poet wherein he said:

"Not a created thing is the Speech of our great King,"

Within this, there is an affirmation of two affairs which are connected to the Attribute of Speech. The first affair is that speech is an Attribute of Allaah; so the Qur'aan is the speech of Allaah and it is not the speech of anyone from the creation. It being attributed to Allaah is from the perspective of attribution of the attribute to the one who has been described with it. In opposition to the Mu'tazilah who say that it is from the perspective of attribution of the creation to the

---

[25] Soorah Al-Baqarah (2:136)

Creator. The things which are attributed to Allaah, the Exalted, are of two types:

Firstly: There are the things which are attributed to Allaah from the perspective of attributing the description to the one who is described with it; such as the Hearing of Allaah, the Sight of Allaah, the Ability of Allaah, the Speech of Allaah, and the Knowledge of Allaah. The guideline of this is that that which is attributed to a description that is not able to stand independently apart from the One that is being described.

Secondly: That which is ascribed to Allaah from the perspective of attributing the creation to its creator; such as the servant of Allaah, the female servant of Allaah, the she-camel of Allah, and the house of Allaah. Its guideline is that that which is ascribed to Allaah in this fashion is able to stand independently in of itself.

This is the state of that which it is said concerning it that it is from Allaah; perhaps it may be a description of Him and perhaps it may be a creation of His.

Allaah, the Exalted has said:

﴿ وَلَٰكِنْ حَقَّ ٱلْقَوْلُ مِنِّى لَأَمْلَأَنَّ جَهَنَّمَ مِنَ ٱلْجِنَّةِ وَٱلنَّاسِ أَجْمَعِينَ ﴿١٣﴾ ﴾

But the Word from Me took effect (about evil-doers), that I will fill Hell with jinn and mankind together. [26]

Speech is a description of the Lord, Glorified be He, and it is an Attribute from amongst His Attributes.

Allaah, the Exalted has said:

﴿ وَسَخَّرَ لَكُم مَّا فِى ٱلسَّمَٰوَٰتِ وَمَا فِى ٱلْأَرْضِ جَمِيعًا مِّنْهُ ﴾

And has subjected to you all that is in the heavens and all that is in the earth; it is all from Him. [27]

So that which is within the heavens and the earth is all from Allaah in terms of creation and His bringing them into existence. In this regard, two groups have gone astray; the Mu'tazilah who attribute all things to Allaah in terms of His creation of them and bringing them into existence in order that they may arrive at

---

[26] Soorah As-Sajdah (32:13)

[27] Soorah Al-Jathiyah (45:13)

their vile statement. And it is the statement that the Speech of Allaah is created.

Likewise, the extremist Sufis since they have made all things attributable to Allaah in terms of His description in order that they may arrive at their foul statement; and it is the statement of *Al-Hulool* (that Allaah is incarnate within all of the creation) as well as Wahdatul-Wujood (unity of existence i.e. everything is Allaah and Allaah is everything) Exalted be Allaah above that which they describe Him with.

The truth is balanced between the two of these and that which is correct is that ascribing Speech to Allaah, the Mighty and Majestic, is from the perspective of ascribing the description to the one who has been described.

When it is said: *"...the speech of our King,"* this comprises an important principle as it relates to the Attributes and it is that that which is ascribed to Allaah from the Attributes is affirmed for Him in a manner befitting to Him and this comprises the statement: *"...the speech of our King,"* Meaning: it is an Attribute of Allaah that is befitting to Him and it does not resemble the attributes of the creation. So He, Glorified be He, has perfection in His Essence and in His Attributes. Due to this, some of the Salaf said:

> "If you want to know the difference between the Speech of Allaah and the speech of the creation, then it is like the difference between the creator and the creation."

The principle according to the people of knowledge is that ascription necessitates specification, and when speech is ascribed to Allaah, then it is specific to Him and it is befitting His Majesty and His Perfection. And when speech is attributed to the creation, then it is specific to them, and it is befitting to their weakness and deficiency. And it is not a necessity that two things which are similar in name also be in agreement with their reality and description. And this is as it relates to the creation and the creation how much more so as it relates to the creation and the Creator.

The second affair is that statement of the poet: *"...not created,"* this contains a refutation and negation of the statement of the one who says that the Speech of Allaah is a creation from the creation which Allaah has brought into existence by way of His Ability. The poet clarifies the falsehood of his creed with his statement: *"...not created,"* The statement that the Qur'aan is created is the creed of the Jahmiyah as well as the Mu'tazilah and other than them. The Jahmiyah explicitly state this, and they say the Qur'aan is created, and the speech is created, and they do not say that it is the Speech of Allaah. Due to this, their

Shaykh tried to distort the statement of Allaah, the Exalted wherein He said:

﴿وَكَلَّمَ ٱللَّهُ مُوسَىٰ تَكۡلِيمٗا ١٦٤﴾

And to Moosaa (Moses) Allaah spoke directly. [28]

He sought to make the name of Allaah accusative in an attempt to flee from attributing speech to Allaah.[29] As for the Mu'tazilah, they attributed speech to Allaah. However, they deem it to be from the perspective of attributing the creation to its Creator.

The Ashaa'irah, as well as the Kullaabiyah, also say that the Qur'aan is created. However, they do not do so explicitly. They say the speech is of two types:

The First: *Kalaam Nafsee,* which is not by way of letters nor sounds; this is that which they attribute to Allaah.

---

[28] Soorah An-Nisā (4:164)

[29] Translator's note: By making Allaah's Name accusative (i.e., placing a Fat'hah on the last letter), this would make Allaah the object of the verb—meaning the one who was spoken to—and Moosaa the doer of the verb—i.e., the one who spoke; thus they tried to misinterpret the statement of Allaah to mean: *And Moosaa spoke to Allaah directly.*

The Second: *Al-Kalam Al-Lafdhee* (uttered speech); this comprises letters and sounds as well as that which is the Qur'aan. Therefore it is created, and it is an expression or report of the speech of Allaah and it is not the speech of Allaah. Rather, it is created just as the rest of the creation. And so by way of this, they are just like the Jahmiyah.

So the poet, with his statement: *"...not created,"* negates all of these statements. Therefore, the Qur'aan is the Speech of Allaah in reality and it is consists of letters and sounds; Jibreel heard it from Allaah, the Mighty and Majestic, and its words and its meanings are the speech of Allaah.

One is not to say that its words are the Speech of Allaah, but not its meanings; nor is one to say that its meanings are the Speech of Allaah but not its words.

The statement of the poet when he said: *"...our King,"* contains the affirmation of the attribute of sovereignty for Allaah. For Allaah is the King of the kingdom and the entire kingdom belongs to Allaah. Allaah, the Exalted has said:

﴿ قُلِ ٱللَّهُمَّ مَٰلِكَ ٱلۡمُلۡكِ تُؤۡتِي ٱلۡمُلۡكَ مَن تَشَآءُ وَتَنزِعُ ٱلۡمُلۡكَ مِمَّن تَشَآءُ
وَتُعِزُّ مَن تَشَآءُ وَتُذِلُّ مَن تَشَآءُۖ بِيَدِكَ ٱلۡخَيۡرُۖ إِنَّكَ عَلَىٰ كُلِّ شَيۡءٖ قَدِيرٞ ٢٦ ﴾

Say (O Muhammad ﷺ): "O Allaah! Possessor of the kingdom, You give the kingdom to whom You will, and You take the kingdom from whom You will, and You endue with honor whom You will, and You humiliate whom You will. In Your Hand is the good. Verily, You are Able to do all things. [30]

If the creation owns a thing, it is only by way of Allaah granting them ownership of it. So Allaah is the owner of the Dunyaa as well as the hereafter. Ownership is from the aspects of Lordship. This is because lordship has several meanings and from them there is the master; the one who is obeyed as well as Ownership.

The statement of the poet when he said: *"Such ..."* is an indication here to that which is preceded by the first portion from the clarification of the correct creed regarding the speech of Allaah.

"Such was the religion of the pious ones," Meaning they had Eemaan, and they believed in that. The pious took as their religion the fact that the Qur'aan is the speech of Allaah and that it is not created. This is their creed which they did not divert from. The transmissions from them in this regard are many. Al-Laalikaa'ee, may Allaah have mercy upon him, formulated a chapter

[30] Soorah Aali Imran (3:26)

within his book; Sharh Al-I'tiqaad in clarification of the fact that the Speech of Allaah is not created and he named more than five-hundred people who mention the same, and some of them narrated this by way of a chain of narration. All of them affirming that the Qur'aan is the Speech of Allaah, and it is not created. And he who says that it is created, then he is a disbeliever. And the transmissions from them in this regard are very many.

As it relates to this, Ibn Al-Qayyim, may Allaah have mercy upon him, said:

> "Five-hundred of the scholars have reported their disbelief in the various lands. Al-Laalikaa'ee, the Imaam, reported it from them. Rather, before him At-Tabaraanee reported it."

The statement of the poet wherein he said: *"...the pious,"* The choice of this description for Ahlus-Sunnah is excellent and precise. For Taqwaa is from the word *Al-Waqaayah* (to shield) by way of the individual placing between himself and that which he fears a shield to protect him. Therefore, the Taqwaa of Allaah is that the individual places between himself and that which he fears from the anger of Allaah and His displeasure a shield to protect him by way of enacting the commands and abandoning the prohibitions.

Due to this the best of that which Taqwaa has been defined is the statement of Talq ibn Habeeb, may Allaah have mercy upon him, wherein he said:

> "Taqwaa is that you act in obedience of Allaah upon light from Allaah hoping for the reward of Allaah and that you abandon disobeying Allaah upon light from Allaah fearing the punishment of Allaah."

Ibn Al-Qayyim, may Allaah have mercy upon him, stated:

> "This is the best of that with which Taqwaa has been defined."

Adh-Dhahabee mentioned within his biography:

> "And he has done well and explained it excellently."

Similarly, Shaykh Al-Islaam indicated this definition, as did Ibn Rajab. So these eminent Imaams—I am referring to the Imaams of Ahlus-Sunnah—all had Taqwaa of Allaah by way of clinging to the Sunan and acts of obedience as well as abandoning the prohibitions and newly invented matters. And the greatest of that which they abandoned and stayed away from was disbelief, innovation, and newly invented matters; and from it is the statement that the

Qur'aan is created. In addition to that which it contains from disbelief and misguidance it also leads to many other forms of corruption and dangers for the one who says it.

Due to this, the statement of the Jahmiyah amounts to belittlement of the Speech of Allaah and the absence of concern for it, because of their claim that it is a creation from the other forms of creation.

The saying of the poet wherein he said: *"...which they clearly expressed,"* meaning: in addition to their taking this as their religion and believing it within their hearts, they spoke eloquently and explicitly regarding it, and they clarified and affirmed it within their gatherings and they spoke eloquently about it and aided it; especially when the people of falsehood outwardly proclaimed their falsehood and explicitly stated their misguidance.

Due to this, it is reported from Aboo Haamid Al-Isfareenee that every Friday he would stand and say:

> "The Qur'aan is the speech of Allaah and it is not created in opposition to the statement of Al-Baaqilnaanee. This is so that no one who comes after us will think that we are upon his creed."

This was because he lived during his time, and this is also reported from Shaykh Al-Islaam within Sharh Al-'Aqeedah Al-Asfahaniyyah. [31]

And this (i.e., their speaking eloquently regarding it) the books of Ahlus-Sunnah have come bearing this meaning. So one will not find a book written on creed except that it contains explicit mention of that and eloquent speech regarding it. Rather, they have even dedicated specific books and writings to this. The poet said:

"And do not be a person who takes no position on the Qur'aan as did the followers of Jahm, and they had been too lax."

After the poet had completed speaking regarding the initial issue, he began refuting a group from amongst the groups of the Jahmiyah and they are the *Waaqifah.* It is known that the Madh'hab of Ahlus-Sunnah is that they would eloquently and explicitly state that the Qur'aan is the speech of Allaah and that it is not created. Whereas the methodology of the Jahmiyah is that they would explicitly state the opposite of that, which is that the Qur'aan is created. And upon the traces of the Aqeedah of the Jahmiyah, the innovation of the *Waaqifah* came about. So those

[31] Refer to Sharh Al-'Aqeedah Al-Asfahaniyyah pg. 36.

who were affected by the innovation of the Jahmiyah, who say that the Qur'aan is created, began to spread this amongst the people, and they circulated these doubts. So Ahlus-Sunnah began to refute them and in this environment arose the *Waaqifah* who were affected by the Jahmiyah and they are the people of doubts. They say that the Qur'aan is the speech of Allaah, and they do not say that it is created nor do they say that it is not created. They only did this due to their being affected by the innovation of the Jahmiyah; and it having entered into their souls. Due to this, they were not able to explicitly state the correct 'Aqeedah, and it is that the Qur'aan is not created. Due to this, Imaam Ahmad said: *"The Waaqifah are Jahmiyah."* The poet also said this when he described them as being *"...followers of Jahm."* Some of the people of knowledge said that they are eviler then the Jahmiyah and this is because the creed of Al-Jahmiyah was explicit in its falsehood, and it is that the Qur'aan is created. Thus criticizing it, clarifying its corruption to the people by way of proofs and evidence is easy. However, since the *Waaqifah* have come and base their Madhhab upon the fact that they take their position from the perspective of piety, and they withhold regarding this issue, then this is more dangerous to the common folk. For they perceive that within their statement there is a form of balance and justness.

What is obligatory is that one explicitly state the correct creed which the Book and the Sunnah indicates and not having Eemaan in it or being hesitant and wavering regarding this issue is all from deviation and misguidance. Allaah, the Exalted, has said:

﴿إِنَّمَا ٱلْمُؤْمِنُونَ ٱلَّذِينَ ءَامَنُوا۟ بِٱللَّهِ وَرَسُولِهِۦ ثُمَّ لَمْ يَرْتَابُوا۟﴾

Only those are the believers who have believed in Allaah and His Messenger, and afterward doubt not. [32]

And hesitating from having Eemaan in the truth is a type of doubt and ambiguity.

The statement of the poet when he said: *"Jahm..."* this is the son of Safwaan, the head of the Jahmiyah. The people of knowledge have mentioned that the origin of this negation is that Jahm took it from Al-Ja'd ibn Dirham who took it from Aaban ibn Sam'aan who likewise took it from Taalut who was the nephew of Labeed who took it from Labeed ibn Al-A'sam the Jew; and he took that from the Jews of Yemen. This is the chain of this misguidance linking back to the Jews. And from this it is known that the basis of *Ta'teel*

---

[32] Soorah Al-Hujurat (49:15)

(negation of the Attributes) is the Jews just as they are the basis for the Raafidah.

The poet, may Allaah have mercy upon him, said: *"and they had been too lax,"* To be lax regarding a thing means: to incline oneself towards it, and the followers of Jahm inclined with themselves, and their hearts leaned towards this creed.

In another manuscript of the same poem it reads: *"...and they permitted it,"* This bears the meaning that their souls permitted believing in this statement and affirming it in spite of its corruption and its falsehood.

Then the poet went on to say: *"And do not say that the Qur'aan is created, as I have recited it..."* meaning: *Do not say that my recitation of the Qur'aan is created.* This contains a refutation against another innovation other than that innovation of the Waaqifah. It is that innovation of the Lafdhiyah who say:

> My articulation of the Qur'aan is created. Meaning: When I recite the Qur'aan, then this is created or my recitation of the Qur'aan is created.

The origin of this innovation is the innovation of the Jahmiyah itself and their doubt is the doubt of the Jahmiyah; because articulation and recitation and reading all originate from one of two affairs:

Firstly: It is that that which is uttered, recited and read; is the Speech of Allaah and this is not created.

Secondly: That which the tongue and the lips and the throat and the voice of the person move with is created. So when it is said: *My articulation of the Qur'aan is created*, then one of these two things is interpreted or understood.

So the Lafdhiyah, as the people of knowledge affirm, are Jahmiyah and their innovating this innovation is similar to affirmation of the methodology of Jahm by way of another path and another method. They do this in order to deceive the people. So when one says: *My articulation of the Qur'aan is created*, then this goes back to the statement of the Jahmiyah who say that the Qur'aan is created.

Due to this, Imaam Ahmad, may Allaah have mercy upon him, as well as other than him all say that the Lafdhiyah are Jahmiyah. Meaning, he who says that his articulation of the Qur'aan is created, then he is speaking with the statement of Jahm.

Imaam Ahmad, may Allaah have mercy upon him, said:

> "He who says that my articulation the Qur'aan is created, then he is a Jahmee. And he who says that it is not created then he is an innovator."

This is because the statement: "My articulation of the Qur'aan is created," bears two affairs; one of them being created which is the movement of the tongue and the other not being created which is the Speech of Allaah; and it is falsehood for one to say that the speech of Allaah, Glorified be He, is created.

So when one says: *"My articulation of the Qur'aan is not created."* Then also this bears two affairs; one of them being the movement of the tongue and it is false that it should be said that this is not created. And the other is that which is recited and read; and this is not created. Due to this, that which is correct is to provide details. So if one intends that which is uttered, then this is the Speech of Allaah and it is not created. And if one intends the movement of the tongue and the throat and the voice of the servant, then this is created. That which is correct is that the voice is the voice of reciter and the speech is the Speech of the creator; and speech is attributed to the one who said it originally and not the one who said it by way of convenience and relaying (that speech). Due to this, Imaam Ahmad said:

"The Qur'aan is the speech of Allaah in every form."

Meaning, whether it is memorized within the chests or written upon parchment or recited upon the tongues or heard with the ears; and the reason for the poet prohibiting the statement of the Lafdhiyah is clear within his statement:

"...Since the Speech of Allaah, through its recitation, is made clear."

And this is the meaning of the statement of Ahlus-Sunnah that the Qur'aan is the speech of Allaah in its words as well as its meanings; and it is not simply the speech of Allaah in its wordings but not its meanings nor in its meanings without its wordings. And the words make clear the meaning and they clarify that what is intended and they elucidate the objectives.

AFFIRMATION OF THE SEEING OF ALLAAH IN THE HEREAFTER

(6) وَقُـلْ يَتَجلَّى اللهُ للخَلْقِ جَـهْـرةً   كَمَا البدْرُ لا يَخْفى وَرَبُّكَ أَوْضَـحُ

(7) وَلَيْسَ بمَوْلُـودٍ وليسَ بِـوَالِـدٍ   وَلَيسَ لهُ شِـبْهٌ تَعَالَى المسَبَّـحُ

(8) وَقَـدْ يُنكِرُ الجَهْميُّ هَـذَا وعِنْدَنَا   بِمِصْـدَاقِ ما قُلْنَـا حَدِيثٌ مُصَرِّحُ

(9) رَوَاهُ جَرِيـرٌ عـن مَقَـالِ مُحـمَّدٍ   فقُـلْ مِثْلَ ما قَدْ قَالَ في ذَاكَ تَنْجَحُ

6. *And say: Allaah will make Himself visible to the creation, openly,*

Just as the full moon is not hard to see, and your Lord (will be seen) more clearly.

7. *And He was not born, nor has He fathered anyone,*

Nor is there anything similar to Him, Exalted be the Glorified One.

8. A Jahmee rejects this, however, we have

As a testimony to the truth of what we say - a Hadeeth that clarifies it.

9. Jareer narrated it, from the words of Muhammad,

So say what he said about that, and you will be successful.

Explanation

The seeing of Allaah in the hereafter is the truth. The Book and the successively narrated Sunnah prove it; and the Muslims are united upon it. None denies the seeing of Allaah except the deviant Jahmiyah and those who have been affected by them.

Some of the Salaf have said:

> "He who denies the seeing of Allaah, deserves to be deprived of it."[33]

The statement of the poet: *"Say..."* is an address directed to the person of the Sunnah and he who

[33] Refer to Radd Ad-Daarimee 'Alaa Bishr Al-Mareesee pg. 19

wants to follow the Sunnah of the Prophet (صَلَّى ٱللَّهُ عَلَيْهِ وَسَلَّمَ) and cling to his command and follow in his footsteps. As for the person of desires, opinions, caprice, and other than this, then he does not give any weight to the Sunnah nor does he care for it nor does he has any concern for it.

So he is saying: *Say, O person of the Sunnah, without hesitating without doubt: "Allaah will make Himself visible..."* Appearance is being manifest and apparent; meaning Allaah will appear before the creation. What is intended by "creation" is the believers. For they are those who will delight in seeing Him on the Day of Judgment and He will ennoble them by way of them looking at Him. Rather, their seeing Him is the most noble of their objectives and the greatest of their goals and aims; and from their supplications is that they say:

اللَّهُمَّ إِنَّا نَسْأَلُكَ لَذَّةَ النَّظَرِ إِلَى وَجْهِكَ وَ الشَّوْق

إِلَى لِقَائِكَ فِي غَيْرِ ضراء مضرة وَ لَا فِتْنَةً مُضِلَّةٍ

"O Allaah, indeed we ask You for the delight of looking at Your Face and the bliss of meeting You without any harm nor calamity that will divert us from this."

This is the Du'aa that is affirmed from the Prophet (ﷺ)[34] It is affirmed from the Hadeeth of 'Ammaar Ibn Yaasir, may Allaah be pleased with him.

As for the disbelievers they will not see Him as is within the statement of Allaah, the Exalted:

﴿ كَلَّآ إِنَّهُمْ عَن رَّبِّهِمْ يَوْمَئِذٍ لَّمَحْجُوبُونَ ١٥ ﴾

Nay! Surely, they (evil-doers) will be veiled from seeing their Lord that Day. [35]

And since the disbelievers being veiled from seeing the Magnificent Lord is a type of punishment, then the believers being allowed to see Him is the noblest gift and the greatest delight.

His statement: *"...openly,"* Means, they will see him directly in plain sight, there being between them and Allaah nothing that will block them from seeing Him.

"As the full moon is not hidden," And the word Al-Badr refers to the moon on the fourteenth night when it is fully illuminated; and when there is no clouds in front of it. So the believers will all see Him and they will not

---

[34] Reported by An-Nasaa'ee within his Sunan no. 1305 and Al-Albaanee graded it Saheeh within Saheeh Sunan An-Nasaa'ee no. 1304.

[35] Soorah Al-Mutaffifin (83:15)

need to crowd or to push each other in order to see him. Likewise they will not be harmed by looking at Him, so there will not occur harm for anyone by way of seeing Him. All of that affirms that seeing Allaah in the hereafter is a reality and it will be done in simplicity and ease. The sun and the moon are seen by the people with their eyes in reality without any difficulty or hardship. The Prophet (ﷺ) said:

إِنَّكُمْ سَتَرَوْنَ رَبَّكُمْ كَمَا تَرَوْنَ الْقَمَرَ

> **"Indeed you shall see your Lord just as you see the moon."**[36]

The letter ك (within the phrase كما) is to denote resemblance, however there is no resemblance here to the Lord with the moon or the sun; Exalted be Allaah above that. The resemblance here is between one vision and another vision. This is because the letter ك is connected to the vision and this is the action of the servant, so therefore the resemblance is between one vision and another vision; and it is not between one thing which is seen and another thing which is seen. So the meaning is: Just as the people are able to see the moon in reality with their eyes and with their

---

[36] Reported by Al-Bukhaaree no. 554 and Muslim no. 633

vision, then similarly they will be able to see Allaah in reality with their eyes and their vision.

The statement of the poet wherein he said: *"Just as..."* the letter ك is to denote resemblance. The word ما is additional. The meaning is that He will be seen just as the full moon is seen. The poet said: *"...and your Lord will be seen more clearly,"* The moon is a creation from the creations of Allaah and along with that the people see it on the full moon night directly and clearly without their being any type of impediments or difficulty. So how about the Lord, the Creator, the Exalted; indeed He will be seen more clearly than everything. The believer will see Him with their eyes in reality.

Concerning the statement of the poet: *"...and your Lord,"* Meaning, O you who are being addressed in this matter He is the Lord of all of the creation. He nurtures them by way of His favors and blessings. They have no Lord other than Him, nor do they have a creator other than him. His Lordship for His creation is of two types; that which is general and that which is specific. As for the general then it is by way of His creation, provision, and giving blessings as well as health and the likes of that. This is from the affairs which are general for the believer as well as the disbeliever; the righteous as well as the wicked. As for the specific Lordship, than it is His nurturing by way of Eemaan, guidance towards obedience and Tawfeeq in worshiping Him alone. This is specific to the believers. The poet said:

"And He was not born, nor has He fathered anyone, Nor is there anything similar to Him, Exalted be the Glorified One,"

The poet mentioned this stanza after affirming the seeing of Allaah in order to clarify by way of it that its affirmation is actual, however it does not necessitate likening Allaah to one who is begotten nor one who begets; nor does it necessitate resemblance for Allaah. This is because Ahlus-Sunnah affirm the Attributes in a manner that is befitting to Allaah, the Exalted, and that which is attributed to Allaah necessitates it being specific to Him. Therefore, the Attributes which are attributed to Allaah are not like the attributes which are attributed to the creation. Hence, when we attribute an attribute to Allaah, then it is befitting the perfection of Allaah and if it is attributed to the creation then it is befitting its weakness and deficiency. From this it is known the statement of negation for Allaah's Attributes (At-Ta'teel) is based upon anthropomorphism (At-Tamtheel) so the denier of Allaah's Attributes reached the level of denial when he likened Allaah to His creation. Therefore, he did not understand from the attribute which is attributed to Allaah except that it is exactly like that which he knows to be for the creation. So every person of *Ta'teel* (negation) operates under this corrupt delusion; as someone mentioned while describing the people of theological rhetoric:

> "They are people who live under delusion thinking that the truth is with them, however the truth is behind them."

This was mentioned by Adh-Dhahabee with regards to Aboo Hayyaan At-Tawheedee, then he said: *"And you are the carrier of their flag."* They say that if we were to affirm the seeing of Allaah in reality, then we would be affirming for Him a body and likenesses with the creation. This is because (according to them) seeing does not occur except to that which has a body, and this is corrupt form of analogy. This is because they made analogy between Allaah and the creation. Due to this, the Salaf said:

> "An analogy is not to be made between Him and His creation."

So the poet mentioned this line of poetry in order to remove speculation which may perhaps come; and this speculation comes by way of the Jahmiyah. As for before them this delusion did not exist. For the companions did not fathom any of this. Meaning, along with the fact that He will be seen on the Day of Judgment, in reality, by way of the vision of the people: *"And He was not born, nor has He fathered anyone."* Meaning: that which is other than Him does not extend out from Him nor does He extend out from anything else. And this is derived from the statement of Allaah, the Exalted:

﴿لَمْ يَلِدْ وَلَمْ يُولَدْ ۝٣ وَلَمْ يَكُن لَّهُۥ كُفُوًا أَحَدٌۢ ۝٤﴾

"He begets not, nor was He begotten; "And there is none co-equal or comparable unto Him." [37]

The poet said: *"Nor is there anything similar to Him,"* meaning: Allaah is free from imperfections and Exalted. Likeness is an example and a similarity and there is no similarity for Allaah or any examples for Him; nor is there a likeness for Him; neither in His names nor in His Attributes or His actions.

Allaah, the Exalted, has said:

﴿لَيْسَ كَمِثْلِهِۦ شَيْءٌ ۖ وَهُوَ ٱلسَّمِيعُ ٱلْبَصِيرُ ۝١١﴾

[37] Soorah Al-Ikhlas (112:3-4)

There is nothing like unto Him, and He is the All-Hearer, the All-Seer. [38]

And Allaah, the Exalted has also said:

﴿هَلْ تَعْلَمُ لَهُۥ سَمِيًّا ﴿٦٥﴾﴾

Do you know of any who is similar to Him?[39]

And Allaah, the Exalted also said:

﴿وَلَمْ يَكُن لَّهُۥ كُفُوًا أَحَدٌ ﴿٤﴾﴾

"And there is none co-equal or comparable unto Him."[40]

And Allaah, the Exalted said:

﴿فَلَا تَجْعَلُوا لِلَّهِ أَندَادًا وَأَنتُمْ تَعْلَمُونَ ﴿٢٢﴾﴾

Then do not set up rivals unto Allaah (in worship) while you know.[41]

Derived from this is the fact that affirmation of the Attributes does not necessitate anthropomorphism; for

---

[38] Soorah Ash-Shura (42:11)

[39] Soorah Maryam (19:65)

[40] Soorah Al-Ikhlas (112:4)

[41] Soorah Al-Baqarah (2:22)

indeed anthropomorphism is another affair other than affirmation of the Attributes.

Imaam Ahmad, may Allaah have mercy upon him, stated:

> "The Mushabbih (one who likens Allaah to His creation) is the one who says that Allaah's Hand is like my hand, and His hearing is like my hearing; whereas Allaah says:

﴿لَيْسَ كَمِثْلِهِۦ شَىْءٌ ۖ وَهُوَ ٱلسَّمِيعُ ٱلْبَصِيرُ ﴿١١﴾﴾

There is nothing like unto Him, and He is the All-Hearer, the All-Seer.[42]

Therefore the one who affirms the Attributes for Allaah in the manner which is befitting to Him is not a Mushabbih; for indeed the Mushabbih is the one who likens the Attributes of Allaah to the Attributes of the creation. Ahlus-Sunnah criticize these Mushabbihah, and they deem their statement to be a statement of disbelief and misguidance. The Mu'attilah (those who negate the Attributes of Allaah) accuse Ahlus-Sunnah of Tashbeeh (likening Allaah to His creation) either because they do not understand their statement or

[42] Soorah Ash-Shura (42:11)

due the fact that they are people who have an evil objective and a corrupt intention.

The statement of the poet: *"Exalted be Allaah,"* means: He is Exalted above having likenesses or similarities i.e. His status is Greatly Exalted and Majestic is His position and Magnificent be He from having a likeness or a similarity; therefore he is absolving Allaah from any of this, and the Highness is derived from His Loftiness and it is to have a high position and it is affirmed for Allaah in His essence, His status, and His Magnificence.

The statement of the poet wherein he said: *"Glorified be He,"* Means that He is absolved (from imperfections) this is because *At-Tasbeeh* within the language means: absolving Allaah from imperfections, and this Tasbeeh is an act of worship which draws one near to Allaah, and the command to do so has come within many places. Rather, there has come incitement and encouragement to increase in Tasbeeh in various times and an abundant reward, and tremendous recompense has been portioned for the one who establishes it.

There has come within the Hadeeth:

مَنْ قَالَ حِينَ يُصْبِحُ : سُبْحَانَ اللهِ وَ بِحَمْدِهِ مِائَةَ مَرَّةً غُفِرَتْ لَهُ ذُنُوبُهُ وَ لَوْ كَانَتْ مِثْلُ زبدِ الْبَحرِ

> **"He who says when he wakes in the morning: 'Glorified be Allaah and praise be to Him.' one-hundred times then his sins will be forgiven for him even if they were similar to the foam of the sea."**[43]

It is also speech which is beloved to Ar-Rahmaan as has come within the Hadeeth:

كَلِمَتَانِ خَفِيفَتَانِ عَلَى اللِّسَانِ ثَقِيلَتَانِ فِي الْمِيزَانِ حَبِيبَتَانِ إِلَى الرَّحْمَنِ : سُبْحَانَ اللهِ وَ بِحَمْدِهِ سُبْحَانَ اللهِ الْعَظِيم

> **"There are two statements that are light upon the tongue, heavy upon the scales and beloved to Ar-Rahmaan; they are 'Glorified be**

[43] Reported by Al-Bukhaaree no. 6405 as well as Muslim no. 2691 from the Hadeeth of Aboo Hurayrah, may Allaah be pleased with him.

> **Allaah and praise be to Him and Glorified be Allaah the Magnificent.'"**[44]

There has come within another Hadeeth:

أَحَبُّ الْكَلَامِ إِلَى اللهِ : سُبْحَانَ اللهِ ، وَ الْحَمْدُ للهِ ، وَ لَا إِلَهَ إِلَّا اللهُ ، وَ اللهُ أَكْبَرُ

> **"The most beloved speech to Allaah is the statement: 'Glorified be Allaah, all praise be to Allaah; none has the right to be worshiped except Allaah, and Allaah is the Greatest.'"**[45]

Absolving Allaah is from everything that is not befitting to Him. As for the Mu'attilah, they understand from At-Tasbeeh to absolve Allaah from Attributes. Due to this, they say: *"Glorified be the one who is absolved from Attributes."* One of the people of knowledge said:

> "Look at the Tasbeeh of the Jahmiyah, how it lead them to At-Ta'teel (negation of Allaah's Attributes)"

---

44 Reported by Al-Bukhaaree no. 6406 as well as Muslim no. 2694 from the Hadeeth of Aboo Hurayrah, may Allaah be pleased with him.

45 Reported by Muslim no. 2307 from the Hadeeth of Samurah ibn Jundub, may Allaah be pleased with him.

Therefore this Tasbeeh (of theirs) leads to this deviation and misguidance.

It is not permissible for the Muslim to absolve Allaah from that which the Messengers brought. It is obligatory to absolve Allaah from which the enemies of the Messengers of Allaah and those who oppose them came with. Due to this, Allaah, the Exalted said:

﴿ سُبْحَٰنَ رَبِّكَ رَبِّ ٱلْعِزَّةِ عَمَّا يَصِفُونَ ﴿١٨٠﴾ وَسَلَٰمٌ عَلَى ٱلْمُرْسَلِينَ ﴿١٨١﴾ ﴾

Glorified be your Lord, the Lord of Honor and Power! (He is free) from what they attribute unto Him! And peace be on the Messengers! [46]

Meaning: may Allaah be absolved from that which the enemies of the Messengers attribute to Him. So He absolved Himself from that which the enemies of the Messengers attributed to Him because it contains within it Tashbeeh and At-Ta'teel, and He sent salutations of peace upon the Messengers due to the safety of that which they said as it relates to Allaah freeing Him from deficiency and defects.

From the names of Allaah is Al-Qudoos and As-Salaam; they are from the names which absolve Him from imperfection; therefore Allaah is absolved from

---

[46] Soorah As-Saffat (37:180-181)

being described with Attributes of deficiency or being described as being deficient in any way. Allaah is absolved, Glorified be He, from being similar to anyone from His creation or from anyone of His creation being likened to Him. Allaah is absolved from being described with anything that is not befitting to Him; as for His Attributes, Glorified and Exalted be He, and then they are befitting His Majesty and His perfection. Therefore, At-Tasbeeh does not negate or do away with them at all.

The poet said: *"A Jahmee rejects this ..."* The Arabic word قد, when used with a present tense verb, bears different meanings based upon the context. At times, it could mean something which occurs infrequently. At times, it means something which occurs abundantly, and at times it bears the meaning of actualization and emphasis. Here what is intended is actualization and emphasis. So he is saying that in reality the statement of the Jahmiyah is one of rejection for the seeing of Allaah. Due to this, Imaam Ahmad, may Allaah have mercy upon him, said:

> "He who denies that Allaah will be seen, and then he is a Jahmee."

The Jahmee is one who has been affected by Jahm Ibn Safwaan, who was the Shaykh of this methodology and the teacher of these people.

The poet said: *"And this..."* this refers to the seeing of Allaah. When he mentioned the statement of the Jahmiyah, he began thereby refuting them and saying: *"We have with us..."* meaning: we Ahlus-Sunnah Wal-Jamaa'ah have with us: *"A statement in affirmation with that which we say."* Meaning, in confirmation of that which we have stated and it is our affirmation of the seeing of Allaah. *"...an explicit Hadeeth that clarifies it,"* It is not conjecture or opinion. Rather, it is by way of text from the Book and the Sunnah.

"Explicit," meaning: it is explicit in its indication for the affirmation of the seeing of Allaah.

In another manuscript it says: *"An authentic Hadeeth,"* meaning it is authentic in being affirmed from the Messenger of Allaah (ﷺ) and both meanings complete each other.

The Hadeeth, which refers to the seeing of Allaah, is authentic being reported by the Imaams; rather it is Mutawaatir. Several of the people of knowledge have textually mentioned this. Shaykh Al-Islaam Ibn Taymiyah, may Allaah have mercy upon him, said:

> "And this Hadeeth is from the most authentic of the Ahaadeeth on the face of the earth and it has been met with acceptance. The scholars are

> unanimously in agreement regarding the Hadeeth as well as the rest of Ahlus-Sunnah."[47]

And it is explicit in affirmation of the seeing of Allaah, Glorified be He. So there does not remain for the one who denies it any room for discussion.

The poet said: *"Jareer narrated it, from the words of Muhammad,"* Meaning; that the noble companion Jareer ibn 'Abdullah Al-Bajalee, may Allaah be pleased with him, reported it from the statement of the Prophet Muhammad (ﷺ). It is within the two Saheehs and other than them from the books of Sunnah.

Al-Bukhaaree and Muslim reported it from Jareer Ibn 'Abdullah Al-Bajalee, may Allaah be pleased with him, that he said:

> "We were sitting with the Prophet (ﷺ) when he looked towards the moon on a full moon night, and he said:
>
> أَمَّا إِنَّكُمْ سَتَرَوْنَ رَبَّكُمْ كَمَا تَرَوْنَ هَذَا الْقَمَرَ لَا تَضَامُونَ فِي رُؤْيَتِهِ فَإِنِ اسْتَطَعْتُمْ أَنْ لَا تَغْلُبُوا عَلَى صَلَاةٍ قَبْلَ طُلُوعِ الشَّمْسِ وَ قَبْلَ غُرُوبِهَا فَافْعَلُوا

[47] Majmoo' Al-Fataawaa 6/421

> **"Indeed you shall see your Lord just as you see this moon on the full moon night, and you will have no difficulty in seeing Him. So if you are able to not allow a prayer to miss you before the rising of the sun and a prayer before its setting, then do so."**

Meaning: Before Fajr and Asr. This is that which the poet is indicating here. The Hadeeth regarding the seeing of Allaah is a Hadeeth, which is Mutawaatir.

It has been reported from the Prophet (صَلَّى اللهُ عَلَيْهِ وَسَلَّمَ) by many of the companions; from them there is Aboo Hurayrah as well as Aboo Musa Al-Ash'aree, and Jaabir ibn 'Abdullah and other than them, may Allaah be pleased with all of them.

It is obligatory to stop at the Ahaadeeth which are affirmed from the Messenger of Allaah (صَلَّى اللهُ عَلَيْهِ وَسَلَّمَ) whether they be Mutawaatir narrations or Aahaad narrations. However, the people of Ta'teel do not give them any weight nor do they pay them any attention. Rather, they shy away from mentioning them, and they reject and refute them.

After the poet mentioned the refutation against the Jahmiyah, he said: *"So say..."* Meaning: O person of the Sunnah, say *"...what he said about that,"* Meaning the Messenger of Allaah (صَلَّى اللهُ عَلَيْهِ وَسَلَّمَ) and do not say that likes of that which the Jahmiyah Al-Mu'attilah negationist say: *"...about that,"* Meaning: As it relates to the seeing of Allaah or as it relates to the Attributes of Allaah in general. It is as if the poet here is laying out a precise methodology which is the path of safety; and it is that the Sunnee should say regarding the Attributes of Allaah just as the Prophet (صَلَّى ٱللَّهُ عَلَيْهِ وَسَلَّمَ) said; and this is the meaning of that which Imaam Ahmad, may Allaah have mercy upon him, said:

> "We describe Allaah with that which He has described Himself with and with that which His Prophet (صَلَّى ٱللَّهُ عَلَيْهِ وَسَلَّمَ) has described Him with, and we do not transgress the Qur'aan and the Ahaadeeth."

The poet said: *"...and you will be successful."* Meaning, by way of this you shall be successful, and success is victory and the attainment of one's objective. Here it means being victorious by gaining the bounty of Allaah and actualizing the correct creed and success by way of happiness in the Dunyaa and the Hereafter.

AFFIRMATION THE ATTRIBUTE OF TWO HANDS FOR ALLAAH THE EXALTED

(١٠) وَقَـدْ يُنكِـرُ الجَهْمِيُّ أَيضًا يَمِينَـهُ وَكِلْتَا يَدَيْـهِ بالفواضِـلِ تَنْفَـحُ

10. And certainly a Jahmee will deny His Right Hand as well,

While both of His Hands are giving out all kinds of bounties.

Explanation

This stanza is set to affirm this magnificent attribute; the attribute of two Hands for Allaah in a manner that befits His Majesty. Ahlus-Sunnah affirm the two Hands for Allaah in reality in the manner that is befitting the perfection of Allaah and His Majesty without likening them to the hands of the creation. Rather, they say Allaah has two Hands which are real and they do not resemble the hands of the creation. This is their affair at it relates to affirming all of the

Attributes. So as it relates to affirmation, they are cautious from two dangerous errors, and they are:

1. At-Ta'teel (negation of Allaah's Attributes)
2. At-Tamtheel (anthropomorphism)

So their methodology, as it relates to the Attributes, is predicated on two principles, and they are Firstly: Affirmation without anthropomorphism. Secondly: absolving Allaah of likenesses and deficiencies without negation of Allaah's Attributes.

Ahlus-Sunnah affirm the Hand for Allaah without likening it to the Attributes of the creation, and they absolve Allaah from deficiency. However, they do so without negating from Him that which they have affirmed from an actual Hand, which is befitting of His Majesty and Perfection. Two deviant methodologies oppose this methodology upon which traverse Ahlus-Sunnah as it relates to the affirmation Allaah's Attributes:

The First is affirmation of them by way of Tamtheel; and these are the Mushabbihah who liken the Attributes of Allaah to the Attributes of His creation. Ahlus-Sunnah are not Mushabbihah, for Tashbeeh is a deviant and disbelieving methodology. This is because he who says concerning his Lord that His Hand is similar to his own hand and that His hearing is similar to his own hearing, and that His sight is similar to his own sight, then he worships an idol from the amongst the different idols and he worships a false deity from amongst the other false deities.

The Second: Absolving by way of negation and these are the Mu'attilah, who reject the Attributes of Allaah and negate them based upon the argument that they are absolving Allaah from likeness with His creation. And they are of various categories. From them, there are those who negate the Names and Attributes. From them, there are those who negate the Attributes but not the Names, and from them there are those who negate some of the Attributes and not others. The one who negates the Attributes of Allaah is the worshiper of nothing. Due to this it is said that the Mushabbih worships and idol while the Mu'attil worships nothing.

These two methodologies and that that which extends from them together fit one comprehensive description, and this is deviation as it relates to the names and Attributes of Allaah. Allaah has commanded us to beware of this methodology and He has threatened its people with the most severe threat within His statement:

﴿ وَلِلَّهِ ٱلْأَسْمَآءُ ٱلْحُسْنَىٰ فَٱدْعُوهُ بِهَا ۖ وَذَرُوا۟ ٱلَّذِينَ يُلْحِدُونَ فِىٓ أَسْمَـٰٓئِهِۦ ۚ سَيُجْزَوْنَ مَا كَانُوا۟ يَعْمَلُونَ ﴿١٨٠﴾ ﴾

And (all) the Most Beautiful Names belong to Allaah, so call on Him by them, and leave the company of those who deviate regarding His Names. They will be requited for what they used to do. [48]

The Mumathilah say regarding the Hand that it is a hand similar to our hands. So they do not affirm for Allaah a Hand which is befitting to Him. The Mu'attilah say that it is required from our affirming a Hand that Allaah has a likeness. Therefore we do not affirm for Allaah a Hand in reality. Due to this, they (the scholars) say:

> "Every Mu'attil is a Mumathil (person of Tamtheel) and every Mumathil is a Mu'attil."

As for the statement: Every Mu'attil is a Mumathil; this is because by way of his Ta'teel (negation) of the Attributes, then he has arrived at Tamtheel. Therefore, they did not reject the hand except due to the delusion that affirming it for Allaah in reality necessitates At-Tashbeeh. Therefore, they negated the hand from

---

[48] Soorah Al-A'raf (7:180)

Allaah. So when he reads the statement of Allaah, the Exalted:

﴿مَا مَنَعَكَ أَن تَسْجُدَ لِمَا خَلَقْتُ بِيَدَيَّ أَسْتَكْبَرْتَ أَمْ كُنتَ مِنَ الْعَالِينَ ﴿٧٥﴾﴾

What prevents you from prostrating yourself to one whom I have created with Both My Hands. Are you too proud (to fall prostrate to Adam) or are you one of the highly exalted? [49]

He does understand from it except the created hand, and this pushes him to absolving Allaah; there is no path, according to him, to absolving Allaah from imperfections except by way of negating this hand from Allaah. And upon this are the general populous of those who negate the Attributes of Allaah and deny them. This is because they did not understand from that which is attributed to Allaah except exactly that which they see and have witness within the creation. Due to this, some of them have an explicitly stated:

> "We did not understand from a hand except exactly that which we see and witness."

Therefore, they fled from evil and fell into evil and something which is more despicable than it.

---

[49] Soorah Sad (38:75)

Moreover, once they negated the Attributes of Allaah as a result of the Tamtheel which they are upon, then they transitioned into another form of Tamtheel and they likened Allaah to non-existent things or inanimate objects, or things which were incapable in accordance to the type of Ta'teel that they performed.

It is apparent from this that every Mu'attil is a Mumathil in two instances; one instance, which is before the Ta'teel and another instance which comes after it. Therefore, every form of Ta'teel gives birth to two forms of Tamtheel. And as it relates to the statement that every Mumathil is a Mu'attil, then he who likens the Attributes of Allaah to the Attributes of His creation, then he is a Mu'attil. And it is not the case that he is a Mu'attil once. Rather he is Mu'attil in three instances. For the one who reads the statement of Allaah, the Exalted:

﴿مَا مَنَعَكَ أَن تَسْجُدَ لِمَا خَلَقْتُ بِيَدَيَّ﴾

What prevents you from prostrating yourself to one whom I have created with Both My Hands? [50]

---

[50] Soorah Sad (38:75)

And then understands from it that the Hand of Allaah is similar to our hands then he has fallen into three forms of Ta'teel.

1. Negating the attribute of an actual hand which is befitting to Allaah and does not resemble the hand of the creation from him.
2. Negating this text and it is the statement of Allaah, the Exalted:

﴿مَا مَنَعَكَ أَن تَسْجُدَ لِمَا خَلَقْتُ بِيَدَيَّ﴾

What prevents you from prostrating yourself to one whom I have created with Both My Hands? [51]

And they negated from that which it indicates. It indicates the affirmation of an actual hand which is befitting to Allaah and they have made it to mean a hand which resembles that hand of the creation.

3. Thirdly, by way of their negating many texts within the Qur'aan that negate likenesses from Allaah; such as the statement of Allaah, the Exalted:

﴿لَيْسَ كَمِثْلِهِۦ شَىْءٌ ۖ وَهُوَ ٱلسَّمِيعُ ٱلْبَصِيرُ ١١﴾

[51] Soorah Sad (38:75)

There is nothing like unto Him, and He is the All-Hearer, the All-Seer. [52]

None is safe from At-Ta'teel and Tamtheel from the various groups with the exception of Ahlus-Sunnah Wal Jamaa'ah. Those other than them are Mu'attilah and Mumathilah at the same time, although all of them claim in that which is apparent from their statements that they are neither a Mu'attil nor a Mumathil.

The poet began by affirming the attribute of a Hand in refutation of the Jahmiyah. The Jahmiyah are the bases of evil and the head of calamities as it relates to negation of the Attributes. Due to this, every Mu'attil is a Jahmee, and every Mu'attil has as his first scholar al-Jahm ibn Safwaan. This is because they have inherited from him the heritage of At-Ta'teel. However, in their taking from him they vary. Some of them take from him a large portion and some of them have taken from him less than that.

The poet said: *"And certainly a Jahmee will deny …"* Meaning, the one traverses upon the methodology of Jahm and is affected by his doubts, obstinately rejects. The word قَدْ here is to show emphasis and actualization. The word أَيضًا means: Along with his

[52] Soorah Ash-Shura (42:11)

rejection of other Attributes. And the statement: "يَمِينِهِ (His Right Hand)," means: the affirmation of the Right Hand and the Hand of Allaah, while the Hand of Allaah is affirmed within the Qur'aan and the Sunnah by way of hundreds of texts; and they have been described with many Attributes such that he who reads those evidences will not be hesitant in affirming it for Allaah. Rather, the Hand has been described with Attributes that reach one-hundred qualities; from them there is folding, grasping, striking, seizing, giving, and other than it from the Attributes, all of them emphasize and affirm this attribute for Allaah in reality; in a manner that is befitting to Him.

Since the affair is like this, then how was Jahm able to embed within the souls of those affected by him the lack of affirming the Hand for Allaah? Before the statement of Jahm everyone who read the verses which spoke about the Attributes within the Qur'aan did not understand from them except the Attributes as they actually were befitting to Allaah. That is known by way of examining the common folk who did not take from a Jahmee nor any person of theological rhetoric. When you recite to them a verse about the Attributes of Allaah, they do not understand from it except the Attribute as it actually is. Jahm reflected on this affair and began formulating absolute principles in order to obstinately reject the Attributes of Allaah. So he was not able to come to the people in the beginning and say to them:

Allaah does not have a hand.

Therefore, he came by way of beautified general speech and absolved Allaah from it, and he made absolving Allaah from them to be an absolute principle according to these people, and this took them to the level of rejection of the Attributes by way of that since he came with the term Al-Jism (body) as well as the term Al-Hayz (space) and the term Al-Jihah (direction) so he said for example: *"Is Allaah a body*?" So he began to affirm that Allaah does not have a body nor is he to be described as being a body. So once this is affirmed and embedded within their souls, he began to affirm within them that which he wanted and said:

> *"If we affirm for Allaah a hand then we have affirmed for Him a body, and we affirm for Him a body then we have likened Him to His creation."*

And by way of this he embedded in them the negation of the Attributes. However, a problem presented itself, and it is the numerous texts from the Book and the Sunnah which contradict that which he affirmed. Therefore, he directed them towards At-Tahreef (distortion of the meanings of the text).

By way of this, Jahm arrived at rejection of the Attributes of Allaah; by way of sucking them into his doubts and embedding within them his misguidance and falsehood due to ignorance and a scanty amount of insight into the religion.

The statement of the poet: *"Right Hand,"* This is an Attribute, which is affirmed for Allaah. So Allaah has two actual Hands and within a narration reported by Muslim, an affirmation of a Hand for Allaah it mentions that they are a right hand and a left hand. From the people of knowledge are those who deem it to be correct that the wording 'left hand' is not affirmed. Rather what is affirmed is the wording 'other' instead of the word 'left'

At any rate, this narration is not contradictory to the statement of the Prophet (صَلَّى اللهُ عَلَيْهِ وَسَلَّمَ) wherein he said:

وَ كِلْتَا يَدِي رَبِّي يَمِين

> **"And both of the Hands of my Lord are right hands."[53]**

This is because the people of knowledge have clarified that what is intended by his statement (صَلَّى اللهُ عَلَيْهِ وَسَلَّمَ)

---

[53] Reported by Muslim no. 1827 from the Hadeeth of 'Abdullah ibn 'Amr ibn Al-'Aas, may Allaah be pleased with them both.

"And both of the Hands of my Lord are right hands,"

Is negation of the idea of deficiency, because perhaps the intellects of some will rush to the notion that the left hand or the other hand is more deficient than the right hand. And the right hand is affirmed for Allaah in the Qur'aan and the Sunnah.

Allaah, the Exalted has said:

﴿ وَمَا قَدَرُوا۟ ٱللَّهَ حَقَّ قَدْرِهِۦ وَٱلْأَرْضُ جَمِيعًا قَبْضَتُهُۥ يَوْمَ ٱلْقِيَـٰمَةِ وَٱلسَّمَـٰوَٰتُ مَطْوِيَّـٰتٌۢ بِيَمِينِهِۦ ۚ سُبْحَـٰنَهُۥ وَتَعَـٰلَىٰ عَمَّا يُشْرِكُونَ ﴿٦٧﴾ ﴾

They made not a just estimate of Allaah such as is due to Him. And on the Day of Resurrection the whole of the earth will be grasped by His Hand, and the heavens will be rolled up in His Right Hand. Glorified is He, and High is He above all that they associate as partners with Him! [54]

Within this verse, there is a refutation and a clarification regarding the Mu'attilah, who have said that affirming the Hand for Allaah necessitates likening Allaah to the creation. So it is said to them:

---

54 Soorah Az-Zumar (39:67)

> *How does the intelligent one understand reflecting upon this verse that it will necessitate from affirming a hand for Allaah in reality likening Allaah to the creation, whereas Allaah described Himself with this Magnificence and with Perfection?*

They are refuted by way of the fact that the agreement of the two things in name does not necessitate that they agree in their reality and description. This is made clear between the creation and the creation; so how about between the Creator and the creation?

The poet said: *"While both of His Hands ..."* In this lies affirming the two hands for Allaah in reality, in the manner that befits Him. This textual mention of Him having two hands has come within the Qur'aan and the Sunnah. Allaah, the Exalted has said:

﴿بَلْ يَدَاهُ مَبْسُوطَتَانِ﴾

Nay, both His Hands are widely outstretched. [55]

And within the Hadeeth there comes the statement:

---

[55] Soorah Al-Ma'idah (5:64)

يَـمِـيـنُ اللهِ مَـلأى لَا يَـغِـيـضُـهَـا نَـفَـقَـة سَـحَّـاء الـلَّـيْـلِ وَ النَّـهَـار أَ رَأَيْـتُـمْ مَـا أَنْـفَـقَ مُـنْـذ خَـلـق الـسَّـمَـوَاتِ وَ الْأَرْض فَـإِنَّـهُ لَـمْ يَـغِـضْ مَـا فِـي يَـمِـيـنِـهِ وَ عَـرْشِـهِ عَـلَـى الْـمَـاءِ وَ بِـيَـدِهِ الْأُخْـرَى الـقـسـط يَـرْفَـعُ وَ يَـخْـفِـضُ .

"The Right Hand of Allaah is full and it is not emptied by spending abundantly in night and day. Do you not see that Allaah has spent since the creation of the heavens and the earth, yet that which is within His Hand has not been exhausted and His throne is above the water and within His other hand lies justice; He raises some and debases others." Reported by Bukhaaree and Muslim[56]

This verse and this Hadeeth are from the strongest of evidences in refutation against those who say that His Hand is in reference to His power. So it is said to them; does Allaah have two powers? And the consensus of the people of Islaam is that Allaah does not have two abilities. And it being explained to be a

[56] Al-Bukhaaree reported it no. 7411 as well as Muslim no. 993 from the Hadeeth of Aboo Hurayrah, may Allaah be pleased with him.

Ni'mah (blessing) as well is rejected. This is because no one says that Allaah has two blessings. Rather, His favors are abundant. What do these people say regarding the Hadeeth? Do they say: *"With His other power,"* or *"with His other blessing,"* or what do they say regarding this?

Affirming the two hands for Allaah does not contradict the fact that the Hand has come within the some of the text in the context of plural as is within the statement of Allaah, the Exalted:

﴿أَوَلَمْ يَرَوْا أَنَّا خَلَقْنَا لَهُم مِّمَّا عَمِلَتْ أَيْدِينَآ أَنْعَـٰمًا فَهُمْ لَهَا مَـٰلِكُونَ ﴿٧١﴾﴾

Do they not see that We have created for them of what Our Hands have created, the cattle so that they are their owners. [57]

Similarly, it has come in the singular context as is seen within the statement of Allaah:

﴿تَبَـٰرَكَ ٱلَّذِى بِيَدِهِ ٱلْمُلْكُ وَهُوَ عَلَىٰ كُلِّ شَىْءٍ قَدِيرٌ ﴿١﴾﴾

Blessed is He in Whose Hand is the dominion, and He is Able to do all things.[58]

---

[57] Soorah Ya-Sin (36:71)

[58] Soorah Al-Mulk (67:1)

This is because the language of the Arabs is broad as it relates to information; at times the dual is referred to as plural or singular. This has come within Qur'aan as seen within the statement of Allaah, the Exalted:

﴿ فَقَدْ صَغَتْ قُلُوبُكُمَا ﴾

Your hearts are indeed so inclined [59]

The Arabs still say: *I saw you with my eye, or I heard you with my ear;* using the singular form for eye and ear. There is no contradiction, therefore, between the various wordings that have come. It is similar therefore to the statement regarding the eye.

The poet said:

"While both of His Hands are giving out all kinds of bounties,"

'Bounties' is the plural of 'bounty', and it refers to good, blessings, nobilities, and gifts. Allaah, the Exalted has said:

﴿ بَلْ يَدَاهُ مَبْسُوطَتَانِ يُنفِقُ كَيْفَ يَشَآءُ ﴾

[59] Soorah At-Tahrim (66:4)

> **Nay, both His Hands are widely outstretched. He spends (of His Bounty) as He wills.** [60]

Muslim reported within his Saheeh from the Prophet (ﷺ) that he said:

إِنَّ الْمُقْسِطِينَ عِنْدَ اللهِ يَوْمَ الْقِيَامَةِ عَلَى مَنَابِر مِنْ نُورٍ عَنْ يَمِينِ الرَّحْمَنِ وَ كِلْتَا يَدَيْهِ يَمِينِ الَّذِينَ يَعْدلُونَ فِي حكمِهِمْ وَ أَهْلِيهِمْ وَ مَا وَلوا

> **"Indeed the equitable people will be with Allaah on the Day of Judgment upon Minbars of light to the right of Ar-Rahmaan, and both of His two hands are right hands. They are those who are just in their rulings and dealings with the people."**

The poet then said: تَنْفَحُ (giving out) The word *An-Nafh* means to give. In some of the manuscripts it reads: تنضح, and *An-Nadh* means to spray or to provide with water. What is intended is that Allaah gives abundantly and bestows favors upon His servants and gives them abundant gifts. As has come within the Hadeeth:

[60] Soorah Al-Ma'idah (5:64)

يَـمِـيـنُ اللهِ مَـلَأَى لَا يَـغِـيـضُـهَـا نَـفَـقَـة سَـحَّـاء الـلَّـيْـلِ وَ الـنَّـهَـار

"The right Hand of Allaah is full. It is not depleted by spending by night and by day..."

The Hand is from the Attributes of Allaah connected to His essence. The poet, when mentioning the rejection of the Jahmiyah for the Hand of Allaah, is indicating by way of that their rejection of the other Attributes of essence such as; His Face, His Foot, His Eye, His Shin, and the likes of that. So His speech contains a refutation against them in their rejection of the rest of the Attributes of essence. This is because their statement regarding the Attributes is the same.

The Attributes of Allaah are of two types:

The First: The Attributes of essence and the guideline regarding them is that they are those which are not removed from Allaah's essence, and they are not connected to the *Mashee'ah* (Will of Allaah)

The Second: The Attributes of action; and they are those which are connected to Allaah's Will. There is no difference according to Ahlus-Sunnah Wal-Jamaa'ah between the Attributes as it relates to affirming them. All of them are the truth and are affirmed for Allaah as they have come; so they are to be believed in just as they have come without distorting the meanings nor negating them, nor questioning the howness of them or anthropomorphism.

AFFIRMING THE ATTRIBUTE OF DESCENSION FOR ALLAAH

(11) وَقُـلْ يَنْـزِلُ الجَبَّارُ فـي كُـلِّ لَيْلَةٍ   بِلا كَيْفَ جَلَّ الواحدُ المتَمَـدِّحُ

(12) إلى طَبَـقِ الدُّنيا يَمُـنُّ بِفَضْلِــهِ   فَتُفْرَجُ أَبْوابُ السَّماءِ وتُفْتَـحُ

(13) يَقولُ : ألا مُسْتغفِـرٌ يَلْـقَ غَافِـرًا   ومُسْـتَمنِحٌ خَـيْرًا ورِزقًا فأمْنَـحُ

(14) رَوَى ذَاكَ قَومٌ لا يُـرَدُّ حَـدِيثَهم   ألا خَابَ قَـوْمٌ كذَّبـوهُم وقُبِّحُوا

11. And say: The Ever-Compelling descends each night,

Without asking how, magnificent is the One God and most worthy of praise.

12. Down to the lowest heaven, granting bounty from His Grace,

As the gates of the heaven are open and spread widely.

13. He says: Is there anyone seeking forgiveness who would like to meet a forgiver?

Or anyone seeking bounties of goodness and provisions so the he can be given?

14. A group have reported this whose reports are not to be rejected,

But sadly some have went wrong and did not believe them, thus disfigured themselves.

Explanation

These stanzas are regarding affirmation of the descension of Allaah every night to the lowest heaven. Ahlus-Sunnah have as their methodology regarding the descension the same as that which is their methodology regarding the rest of the attributes. Every attribute which Allaah has and is affirmed within the Book and the Sunnah that Ahlus-Sunnah take them as they have come, and they affirm them for Allaah as He has affirmed them for Himself. Likewise, as His Messenger (ﷺ) has affirmed them for Him.

No one from Ahlus-Sunnah precedes Allaah and His Messenger in statement by saying, after the affirmation of Allaah for His attribute: *This attribute is not befitting for You, O Allaah*; or after the affirmation of the Messenger (ﷺ) of this attributes, they do not say: *This is not befitting of Allaah*, and thus negate from Allaah the attributes; absolving Him from that which He has described Himself with and that which His Messenger (ﷺ) has described Him with as if he is more knowledgeable than Allaah regarding Himself; or as if he is more knowledgeable of Allaah than the Messenger (ﷺ). Exalted be Allaah above that which they say and Glorified be Allaah beyond that which they describe Him with.

Due to this, Ahlus-Sunnah say that it is a must that three principles be observed for the one who wishes to occupy himself with the Names and Attributes.

The First: He affirms within himself that no one is more knowledgeable of Allaah than Allaah. As Allaah has said:

﴿ قُلْ ءَأَنتُمْ أَعْلَمُ أَمِ ٱللَّهُ ﴾

Say, "Do you know better or does Allaah? [61]

[61] Soorah Al-Baqarah (2:140)

The Second: No one from the creation is more knowledgeable of Allaah than the Messenger of Allaah (ﷺ). He is the most knowledgeable of the creation regarding Allaah. As Allaah has said:

﴿ وَمَا يَنطِقُ عَنِ ٱلْهَوَىٰٓ ۝٣ إِنْ هُوَ إِلَّا وَحْىٌ يُوحَىٰ ۝٤ ﴾

> **Nor does he speak of (his own) desire. It is only an Inspiration that is inspired.** [62]

The Third: As it relates to us, Allaah is from the unseen. We do not see Him. So there is no room for a person to delve deep into that which is unseen by him, except by way of revelation. Based upon this, the correct path as it relates to the attributes is that we describe Allaah with that which He has describes Himself with and with that which His Messenger (ﷺ) has described Him with, and we do not transgress the Qur'aan and the Hadeeth. As has been stated by Al-Awzaa'ee, may Allaah have mercy upon him wherein he said:

> "We follow the Sunnah wherever it goes."

Meaning, in terms of negation and affirmation.

---

[62] Soorah An-Najm (53:3-4)

So he in whose hearts those principles are affirmed is prevented from delving deep into the attributes with that which he does not know. He knows the corrupt nature of the methodology of the people of false theological rhetoric who give precedence to their corrupt opinions and intellects over Allaah and His Messenger (ﷺ).

The Sunnah has reported the descension of Allaah and the Hadeeth regarding it has been successively narrated from the Prophet (ﷺ) by twenty-eight companions. This means that the Prophet (ﷺ) on numerous occasions said the statement:

يَنْزِلُ رَبُّنَا إِلَى السَّمَاءِ الدُّنْيَا

"Our Lord descends to the lowest heaven."[63]

And he, (ﷺ) is the most eloquent of the people, and the most articulate of them and the most sincere from amongst them. He conveyed that which was revealed to him in the most eloquent manner and he clarified with the most excellent form of clarification and the clearest of them, and he is the best of the creation of Allaah in terms of absolving Allaah from imperfections and respect for Him. He said on

[63] Reported by Al-Bukhaaree no. 7494 and Muslim no. 758 from the Hadeeth of Aboo Hurayrah, may Allaah be pleased with him.

numerous occasions: ***"Our Lord descends."*** His affirming this attribute for his Lord does not negate his absolving Him of imperfections.

So what will those say who negate the attributes of Allaah and turn away from the statement of Allaah and His Messenger (صلى الله عليه وسلم) and place themselves forward before Allaah and His Messenger (صلى الله عليه وسلم). As for the companions and the Taabi'oon as well as the Imaams of the Salaf, then it is not transmitted from a single one of them that he said that this is not befitting for Allaah or that this is not to be taken upon its apparent meaning. As for those who interpret the meaning of this attribute and say that it is not befitting to Allaah and that it is not to be taken upon its apparent meaning, and are negationist Jahmiyah and those who are sympathetic with them, then they say that Allaah does not descend. Because (according to them) if we affirm for Allaah descension, then we have affirmed for him movement and a place. And this negates from Allaah the attribute of descension.

These forms of intellectual justification emanate from corruption within the heart of these people and from it springs forth their rejection of the attributes. This is drawing a comparison between the Creator and the creation, or it is understanding the attributes with which the Creator has been described in a similar fashion that one understands the attributes with which the creation is described. So they say that if we affirm for Allaah descension then we have affirmed for Him movement, transition, and a place. These affairs are from the incidents and, Allaah is absolved from incidents. The end result, therefore, is negation of this Attribute.

It is said to them: If this justification of yours were correct, then why did the Prophet (صَلَّى اللَّهُ عَلَيْهِ وَسَلَّمَ) say on many occasions: ***"Or Lord descends."*** These people of theological rhetoric will respond by saying that the Prophet (صَلَّى اللَّهُ عَلَيْهِ وَسَلَّمَ) did not intend with his statement the descending of Allaah; he only intended the descending of the angel. But it is said to them that if this were the case; then this speech of the Prophet (صَلَّى اللَّهُ عَلَيْهِ وَسَلَّمَ) is closer to being a riddle or a play on words then it is to being eloquence and clarification.

If the speech of these people were factual, then it would have been binding upon the Prophet (صَلَّى اللَّهُ عَلَيْهِ وَسَلَّمَ) to explicitly say: *"The angel of our Lord descends."* However, he did not do this even once. Each time he said: ***"Our Lord descends."*** If their speech were correct, then he would have said even in one sitting: *"The angel of our Lord descends,"* in order that the absolute speech would be interpreted based upon the restricted speech. However, he did not do this.

This statement of theirs, without doubt, contains revilement of the knowledge of the Prophet (ﷺ) and his eloquence as well as revilement of his sincerity. Because it is said to them: *This which you are saying, did the Prophet know it or not?* And if they say: *He did not know it, however, we know it while he didn't*; then this is considering the Messenger (ﷺ) to be ignorant. And if they say that he knew this affair (ﷺ) then it is said to them:

> Then if he knew it was he not able to eloquently say this and clarify it to the Ummah with the utmost clarity or was he not able?

If they say that he was not able to clarify it to them with eloquence and articulately speak regarding it, however, the Jahmiyah were, then this contains revilement of his eloquence and his clarification. And if they say that he was able to eloquently speak regarding it, then it is said to them that this contains revilement of his sincerity because he knew it and was able to clarify it but in spite of this he did not speak about it. Because he did not say, even once, that the angel of our Lord descends. And if they say that he was sincere to the Ummah and clarified the affairs to them, then it is said to them; then give us even one Hadeeth wherein the Prophet (ﷺ) said:

"The angel of our Lord descends."

These three affairs can be said with regards to the one who negates any attribute from the attributes of Allaah; moreover the Hadeeth itself is a refutation against this form of interpretation, as shall come.

The poet, may Allaah have mercy upon him, affirms the descension of Allaah in a manner that befits His Majesty, Mighty and Majestic be He. Ahlus-Sunnah, as it relates to Allaah's descension, stay away from two affairs: **The First:** Negation of the descension and denial of it. **The Second:** Questioning the howness of the descension. This is based upon the principle of affirmation without anthropomorphism and absolving without negation.

The poet said: *"Say..."* This is an address to the person of the Sunnah and the Salafee creed. It means: *Say this without hesitation or doubt. Rather, say it as a believer in it with certainty.* This is because this statement was said by the Prophet (صَلَّىٰ ٱللَّٰهُ عَلَيْهِ وَسَلَّمَ) in more than one setting. So if you were to say that than you have done no more than say that which the Prophet (صَلَّىٰ ٱللَّٰهُ عَلَيْهِ وَسَلَّمَ) said and you have done no more than believe in the likes of that which the Prophet (صَلَّىٰ ٱللَّٰهُ عَلَيْهِ وَسَلَّمَ) believed. This stanza comprises two principles and within his statement: *"Al-Jabbaar descends every night,"* lies protection from negation. And within his statement: *"Without asking how, Majestic be the One God..."* lies protection from questioning the exact nature of the attributes, and in negation of questioning the exact nature of the attributes lies negation of anthropomorphism. This is because the Mumathil is also a *Mukayyif*. Due to this it is said:

> "Every Mumathil is a Mukayyif (one who questions the exact nature of the attributes) but not every Mukayyif is a Mumathil."

This is because the Mumathil says that Allaah descends like the descension of the creation. While at the same time he describes the exact nature of Allaah's attributes by making them similar to the attribute of the creation. However, not every Mukayyif is a Mumathil because Takyeef occurs by way of anthropomorphism, and perhaps it can also be without anthropomorphism; simply by imagining something within one's mind.

The poet said: *"Without questioning the exact nature..."* what is intended by the poet with this statement is without an exact nature that is known to us. For it is negation of our knowledge for the exact nature of Allaah's attributes and not a negation of it having an exact nature. This is because that which has no exact nature does not exist. For the attributes of Allaah have a description and Allaah knows best how they are.

Due to this Imaam Maalik, may Allaah have mercy upon him, said: *"The exact nature of Allaah's attributes is unknown."* And he did not say: "The exact nature is non-existent."

Knowledge of the exact nature of the attributes is a branch of knowledge of the exact nature of Allaah's essence. So if the Jahmee were to say to you: *How does Allaah descend to the lowest heaven?* Then you say: *What is the exact nature of his essence?* And if he says: *I do not know how it is.* Then it is said to him: *Likewise we do not know the exact nature of His descension.* For the knowledge of the description of Allaah's Attributes requires knowledge of the description of the One who is being described and it is a branch of it and extends out from it.

Ahlus-Sunnah say that Allaah descends to the lowest heavens just as the Messenger of Allaah (ﷺ) has informed and they do not seek to describe its exact nature. So they do not make the attributes of Allaah similar to the attributes of the creation; nor do they make up a description within their minds. The Mu'attilah who negate the descension of Allaah only negate it after making an example its exact nature, because the descension of the creation is solidified within their minds. And this which they have understood with their intellects they assume that Ahlus-Sunnah affirm it and thus accused them of likening Allaah to His creation. Some of them slander Shaykh Al-Islaam by saying that he descended from the Minbar and said: *"Allaah descends just like the descension of mine."* This was stated by Ibn Batootah within his book *Ar-Rihlah.* This is a lie, and it is slander against him, may Allaah have mercy upon him; because Shaykh Al-Islaam was in prison during the time that Ibn Batootah passed by Damascus. The one who desires to know the creed of the Shaykh should read his book: *Sharh Hadeeth An-Nuzool.* He has affirmed within it the falsehood of likening the descension of Allaah to the descension of the created beings within numerous places. And that which led these people to this slander against Shaykh Al-Islaam and other than him, is the fact that they did not understand from the descension except the descension of the creation and once they saw Ahlus-Sunnah affirming this descension they, therefore, describe them as being people who liken Allaah to His creation. May Allaah protect them from likening Him to His creation.

The poet said: *"Al-Jabbaar"* this is a reference to Allaah, and it is a name from His Names just as it is within the statement of Allaah, the Exalted:

﴿ هُوَ ٱللَّهُ ٱلَّذِى لَآ إِلَٰهَ إِلَّا هُوَ ٱلْمَلِكُ ٱلْقُدُّوسُ ٱلسَّلَٰمُ ٱلْمُؤْمِنُ ٱلْمُهَيْمِنُ ٱلْعَزِيزُ ٱلْجَبَّارُ ٱلْمُتَكَبِّرُ ۚ سُبْحَٰنَ ٱللَّهِ عَمَّا يُشْرِكُونَ ﴿٢٣﴾ ﴾

He is Allaah than Whom none has the right to be worshipped, the King, the Holy, the One Free from all defects, the Giver of security, the Watcher over His creatures, the All-Mighty, (Al-Jabbaar) the Compeller, the Supreme. Glory be to Allaah! (High is He) above all that they associate as partners with Him. [64]

And the Jabr which is within His name Al-Jabbaar indicates rectification.

It is said: *"His broken ligament was rectified,"* meaning that it was healed, and it is also said: *"The state of the poor person was rectified,"* meaning that is was made upright.

---

[64] Soorah Al-Hashr (59:23)

And from its indications as well is loftiness and compelling power; meaning that Allaah is High Exalted above His creation, and He has compelling power over His servants.

The term جلّ means: Majestic is His status above At-Takyeef; whether that be based upon ones imagination or comparison with the attributes of the creation.

Allaah, the Exalted, has said:

﴿ تَبَٰرَكَ ٱسْمُ رَبِّكَ ذِى ٱلْجَلَٰلِ وَٱلْإِكْرَامِ ٧٨ ﴾

Blessed be the Name of your Lord (Allaah), the Owner of Majesty and Honor. [65]

The Poet said: *"...the One God,"* Meaning: the one who is singled out with attributes of perfection and descriptions of majesty.

The poet said: *"...and most worthy of praise,"* The word المتمَدّح is a description for the one God; meaning He is the one who the believers praise and laud. For He is the One, who bestows upon the servants favors, and He gives them blessings which obligate that they praise him and that they laud Him in an excellent manner and extol Him.

---

[65] Soorah Ar-Rahman (55:78)

He, Majestic and High be He, is such that no one can enumerate the praises that are due to Him; and He, Glorified be He, is praised and lauded by way of His beautiful Names and lofty Attributes. And He is praised for His favors and blessings which cannot be counted or enumerated.

The poet said:

"...down to the lowest heaven granting bounties from His grace as the gates from the heaven are opened and spread widely."

This sentence within this stanza completes the stanza which preceded. And this is similar to the statement of the Prophet (صَلَّى اللَّهُ عَلَيْهِ وَسَلَّمَ)

"Our Lord descends to the lowest heaven..."

Therefore, the preposition and the genitive clause within his statement: *"...to the lowest heaven,"* is connected to his statement: *"Al-Jabbaar descends..."* the word *Tabaq* is a covering and the sky is a covering for the earth. And every heaven is a covering for the heaven that is beneath it.

Samaa Ad-Dunyaa (the heavens of the earth) is called this due to its closeness to the earth.

The poet said: *"Granting bounties..." Al-Mann* refers to giving and exerting. So Allaah descends in order to give and to bestow favors upon His servants of goodness in various types of blessings.

The poet said: "*As the gates of the heavens are opened and spread widely.*" His statement: *"opened"* means that they are split and opened up. The heavens have doors; what indicates this are many texts. From them the statement of Allaah, the Exalted:

> **For them, the gates of heaven will not be opened** [66]

There has come within some of the narrations of the Hadeeth of Allaah's descent that the doors of the heavens are opened up at the time of the divine descent. Within Musnad of Imaam Ahmad on the authority of Ibn Mas'ood, may Allaah be pleased with him, it is mentioned that the Messenger of Allaah (ﷺ) said:

إِذَا كَانَ ثُلُثُ اللَّيْلِ الْبَاقِي يَهْبِطُ اللهُ عَزَّ وَ جَلَّ إِلَى

السَّمَاءِ الدُّنْيَا ثُمَّ تفْتَحُ أَبْوَاب السَّمَاءِ ثُمَّ يَبْسُطُ

[66] Soorah Al-A'raf (7:40)

يَـدهُ ا فَـيَـقُـولُ : هَـلْ مَـنْ سَـائِـل يـعـطى سـؤله ؟ فَـلَا يَـزَالُ

كَـذَلِـكَ ا حَـتَّـى يَـطـلـع الْـفَـجَـر

"When a third of the night remains, Allaah, the Mighty and Majestic, descends to the lowest heaven then the doors of the heavens opened and He is extends His Hand and says: 'Is there anyone asking so that he may be given that which he requests.' And He continues to be in this state until the dawn appears."[67]

The poet said: *"...and he says,"* meaning Allaah, the Glorified and Exalted, says when He descends. So the one who says the statement is Allaah. For it is not correct that one say that the angel says:

> *"Who is seeking my forgiveness, who is asking of Me, who is supplicating to me?"*

This clarifies the falsehood of the statement of the Jahmiyah wherein they said that the one who descends is the angel. This is because if it were that the one who descends was the angel, then he would have said:

---

67 Reported by Imam Ahmad within Al-Musnad no. 3672.

"Indeed Allaah forgives sins; so who is seeking His forgiveness."

As has come within the other Hadeeth which reads:

إِذَا أَحَبَّ اللهُ الْعَبْدَ نَادَى جِبْرِيلَ إِنِّي أَحَبُّ فُلَانًا فَأَحِبَّهُ فَيحِبُّهُ جِبْرِيلُ وَ يُنَادِي أَهْلَ السَّمَاءِ إِنَّ اللهَ يُحِبُّ فُلَانًا فَأَحِبُّوهُ .

"When Allaah loves a servant He calls out to Jibreel and says: indeed I love so and so, so therefore love him, and thus Jibreel loves and announces to the people of the heavens: 'Indeed Allaah loves so and so therefore love him.'"[68]

There has come within some of the narrations of the Hadeeth of descent that Allaah says:

لَا أَسْأَلُ عَنْ عِبَادِي أَحَدًا غَيْرِي

"I do not ask regarding My servants anyone other than Myself."[69]

---

[68] Reported by Al-Bukhaaree no. 6040 and Muslim no. 2637 from the Hadeeth of Aboo Hurayrah, may Allaah be pleased with them.
[69] Reported by Ahmad no. 16316.

This proves false the statement of these Jahmiyah. This is because it is not possible that this be said by anyone other than Allaah.

The poet said: *"Is there anyone seeking forgiveness…"*

The word ألا is a tool of encouragement. So He is encouraging towards seeking forgiveness and seeking pardon. *Al-Mustagfir* is the one who seeks forgiveness.

The poet said: *"…who would like to meet a Forgiver…"* This is Allaah, the Oft-Forgiving the Possessor of Mercy, Glorified and Exalted be He.

Allaah says:

﴿وَمَن يَغۡفِرُ ٱلذُّنُوبَ إِلَّا ٱللَّهُ﴾

And who can forgive sins but Allaah? [70]

The poet said: *"…or anyone seeking bounties,"* This is one who seeks favors and blessings. The meaning is: *Is there anyone asking Allaah for good and for provisions*? And the good comprises many affairs.

The poet said: *"…so he could be given,"* Meaning; that Allaah may give him that which he needs and grant him that which he asks for. For indeed Allaah's

---

[70] Soorah Aali Imran (3:135)

treasures are plentiful, and they are not exhausted by way of His spending. Allaah, the Exalted has mentioned within the Hadeeth Qudsee:

يَا عِبَادِي لَوْ أَنَّ أَوَّلَكُمْ وَ آخِرَكُمْ وَ إِنْسَكُمْ وَ جِنَّكُمْ قَامُوا فِي صَعِيدٍ وَاحِدٍ فَسَأَلُونِي فَأَعْطَيْتُ كُلَّ إِنْسَانٍ مِنْهِمْ مَسْأَلَتَهُ مَا نَقَصَ ذَلِكَ عِنْدِي إِلَّا كَمَا يَنْقُصُ الْمِخْيَطُ إِذَا دَخَلَ الْبَحر

"O My servants if the first of you and the last of you; the human of you and the Jinn of you; were to stand on one elevated plane and ask of Me and I would to give each individual from amongst them that which he asks for; that will not decrease My kingdom at all except the likes of that which the needle decreases the ocean when it is dipped into it."[71]

Then the poet, may Allaah have mercy upon him, cited the evidence for the descension. He said: *"A group has reported this whose reports are not to be rejected."* The demonstrative pronoun within his statement: ذَاكَ is an

---

[71] Reported by Muslim no. 2577 from the Hadeeth of Aboo Dharr may Allaah be pleased with him.

indication to the affirmed divine descension. Meaning; those who have narrated the Hadeeth of the descension are trust worthy and firm, and their narrations are not to be rejected. Rather, they are to be met with acceptance. The Hadeeth is Mutawaatir. It is textualized by more than one of the Imaams. From them is Shaykh Al-Islaam within his book Sharh Hadeeth *An-Nuzool*; as well as Ibn Al-Qayyim within his book *Sawaa'iq Al-Mursalah*; and Adh-Dhahabee within his book Al-'Uloo; as well as As-Suyootee within his book *Al-Azhaar Al-Mutanathirah*; and Al-Kattanee. Ibn Al-Qayyim has mentioned within his book *Al-Sawaa'iq* that twenty-eight companions narrated it, and he mentioned their names.

The poet said: *"but sadly..."* here the term ألا is a tool of commencement and alert; meaning that those who have denied these trustworthy narrators who have reported the descension from the Prophet (صَلَّىٰ اللَّهُ عَلَيْهِ وَسَلَّمَ) were destroyed. And these who have belied the companions in these affairs accept their Ahaadeeth regarding the legislative rulings. So why do they make a distinction?

'Abbaad ibn 'Awwam said:

> "Shurayk came to us and we asked him regarding the Hadeeth: 'Indeed Allaah descends

> on the middle night of Sha'baan.'[72] We said: 'Indeed a people denied these Ahadeeth.' He said: 'What do they say?' We said: 'They revile them.' He said: 'Indeed those who have come with these Ahadeeth are the same ones who have brought the Qur'aan and the Salah and the Hajj and fasting. Allaah is not known except by way of these Ahaadeeth.'"

This misguidance is predicated upon the principle which the Mu'tazilah have instituted and it is that the Aahaad report is not accepted in the field of Aqeedah; while at the same time the Hadeeth of the descension is Mutawaatir. So what guidelines are they adhering to?

He who reflects upon this affair will find that the guideline according to them, is that every Hadeeth which opposes their methodology they reject it with the argument that it is an Aahaad narration; even if the Hadeeth is Mutawaatir. And every Hadeeth which coincides with their desires they accept it even if it is a lie. Due to this, they have depended upon the false Hadeeth: *"The first of that which Allaah has created was the intellect."* And they people are people of desires.

---

[72] Reported by At-Tirmidhee no. 739 and its chain of narration is weak.

The poet, may Allaah mercy upon him, did not mention the highness and the rising above the Throne, however, within the lines of poetry that he has mentioned there is an indication to that, so he sufficed with it. Because in affirmation of the descension also lies affirmation of the highness of Allaah. Due to this, Imaam Adh-Dhahabee cited this poem in totality within his book Al-'Uloo in the context wherein he transmitted from the Imaams that which they have stated in affirmation of the highness of Allaah above His creation.

It is has previously been mentioned the statement of the poet wherein he said: *"Exalted be the Most Glorious (i.e. Allaah),"* and that it contains affirmation of the highness for Allaah, the Exalted, in His Essence, in His Status, as well as His compelling power over His creation. There shall come as well the statement of the poet: *"The possessor the Throne forgives graciously..."*and in this lies affirmation of the magnificent Throne which the Lord, Mighty and Majestic be He, rose above.

THE CREED OF AHLUS-SUNNAH REGARDING THE COMPANIONS

(15) وَقُلْ إنَّ خَيْرَ النَّاسِ بَعْدَ مُحَمَّدٍ وَزِيراهُ قُدْمًا ثُمَّ عُثْمَانُ أرْجَحُ

(16) وَرابِعُهُم خَيْرُ البريَّةِ بَعْدَهُم عَلِيٌّ حَليفُ الخَيرِ بالخَيرِ مُنْجِحُ

(17) وإنَّهمُ و الرَّهْطُ لا رَيْبَ فِيْهِمُ عَلَى نُجُبِ الفِرْدَوْسِ في الخُلْدِ تَسْرَحُ

(18) سَعِيدٌ وسَعْدٌ وابنُ عَوْفٍ وطَلْحةٌ وعَامِرُ فِهْرٍ والزُّبَيْرُ المُمَدَّحُ

(19) وَقُلْ خَيْرَ قولٍ في الصَّحابةِ كُلِّهِمْ ولا تَكُ طَعَّاناً تَعِيْبُ وَتَجْرَحُ

(20) فَقَدْ نَطَقَ الوَحْيُ المُبينُ بِفَضْلِهِمْ وفي الفَتْحِ آيٌ في الصَّحابةِ تَمْدَحُ

15. And say: Indeed the best of the people after Muhammad

Were his two foremost deputies, and then Uthmaan, according to the most correct position.

16. And the fourth of them was the best of creation after them,

'Alee, the companion of goodness, through goodness he was successful.

17. Those are the people, those who we have no doubt about,

Upon the great camels of Firdaws, shining brightly and roaming about.

18. Sa'eed, Sa'd, Ibn 'Awf, Talhah,

Aamir of Fihr, and Zubayr the praiseworthy.

19. And speak with the best terms about the Companions, all of them,

And do not be one who speaks ill of them, pointing out their faults and criticizing,

20. Since the clear Revelation has spoken of their excellence,

And in (Soorah) al-Fat'h are verses about the Companions, praising them.

Explanation

This is summary of the creed of Ahlus-Sunnah regarding the companions. While the poem is, in fact, a summary, the poet has mentioned a great deal. He began this by mentioning the levels of virtue between them, may Allaah be pleased with all of them.

The poet said: "*Say...*" Meaning, O person of the Sunnah, O he who wants the correct creed for himself; the creed of Ahlus-Sunnah and the saved sect and the victorious group, then say while having an open chest, having no doubt or speculation concerning it *"Indeed the best of people after Muhammad..."* meaning, the best of the people and the purest of them after Muhammad (ﷺ) Here the poet affirms that they are the best of the Ummah of Muhammad (ﷺ). So he is saying that the best of the people after Muhammad (ﷺ) are "*...his two foremost deputies*," and they are: Aboo Bakr and 'Umar, may Allaah be pleased with them.

The deputy in the Arabic language is a helper for a king and the one who carries his burdens and consults with him and assists him. Due to this, the poet described Aboo Bakr and 'Umar as being the two deputies for him (صَلَّى ٱللَّهُ عَلَيْهِ وَسَلَّمَ).

The poet said: *"...foremost,"* this is a noun which denotes a time of old. The meaning is that they are two deputies to him and have been since the beginning of his Da'wah. This is because they aided the Prophet (صَلَّى ٱللَّهُ عَلَيْهِ وَسَلَّمَ) from aforetime.

There has come within a Hadeeth that is attributed to the Prophet (صَلَّى ٱللَّهُ عَلَيْهِ وَسَلَّمَ) within At-Tirmidhee and Al-Haakim, that the Prophet (صَلَّى ٱللَّهُ عَلَيْهِ وَسَلَّمَ) said:

> **"There is no prophet except that he had two deputies from the people of the earth and two deputies from the people of the heavens. The two deputies from the heavens are Jibreel and Mikael. And the two deputies from the earth are Aboo Bakr and 'Umar."**[73]

However, the Hadeeth is weak, and it has two other weak chains of narration. But, other Ahadeeth affirm their virtue and the fact that they are the best. Al-Bukhaaree and Muslim reported from the Hadeeth of

---

[73] Reported by At-Tirmidhee no. 3680 and Al-Haakim within Al-Mustadrak 2/290 and he said: "Its chain of narration is Saheeh, although the two Shaykhs did not report it." Al-Albaanee declared it to be weak within Dha'eef Sunan At-Tirmidhee no. 3680.

'Amr ibn Al-'Aas, may Allaah be pleased with him, that he asked the Prophet (ﷺ) saying:

> "Who from amongst the people are the most beloved to you?" He said: **"'Aa'ishah,"** I said: **"Who from amongst the men?"** He said: **"Her father."** I said: "And then whom?" He said: **" Umar ibn Al-Khattaab."** [74]

And they are not simply the best of this Ummah; rather, they are the best of mankind after the prophets and messengers as has come within the Hadeeth:

أَبُو بَكْرٍ وَ عُمَرُ سَيِّدَا كهولِ أَهْلِ الْجَنَّةِ مِنَ الْأَوَّلِينَ

وَ الْآخِرِينَ إِلَّا النَّبِيِّينَ وَ الْمُرْسَلِينَ

> **"Aboo Bakr and 'Umar and the chiefs of the mature men from the people of paradise from the first and the latter people with the exception of the prophets and messengers."**

It has been reported by way of more than one of the companions and from amongst them was 'Alee ibn Abee Taalib, Anas ibn Maalik, Jaabir and Aboo Sa'eed,

[74] Reported by Al-Bukhaaree no. 3662 and Muslim no. 2384.

and it is a Hadeeth which is Saheeh by way of bringing together its various routes of transmission.[75]

It is affirmed within Saheeh Al-Bukhaaree on the authority of Ibn 'Umar, may Allaah be pleased with him, that he said:

> **"During the time of the Prophet (صَلَّى ٱللَّهُ عَلَيْهِ وَسَلَّمَ) we did not deem anyone to be the equivalent of Aboo Bakr and then 'Umar and then 'Uthmaan and then he would leave (remain silent regarding) the (rest of) the companions of the Messenger of Allaah (صَلَّى ٱللَّهُ عَلَيْهِ وَسَلَّمَ) and not deem there to be precedence amongst them."**[76]

It is has been reported by Al-Bukhaaree on the authority of Muhammad ibn Al-Hanafiyyah that he said:

> "I said to my father-meaning 'Alee ibn Abee Taalib-may Allaah be pleased with him, 'Who from amongst the people are the best after the Messenger of Allaah (صَلَّى ٱللَّهُ عَلَيْهِ وَسَلَّمَ).' He said: **'Aboo Bakr'** I said: **'And then whom?'** He said: **''Umar.'"** He (the narrator) said: **"And I was afraid that he would say 'Uthmaan, so I said:**

---

[75] Refer to As-Silsilah As-Saheehah no. 824.

[76] Reported by Al-Bukhaaree no. 3655.

> **'And then you?'** He said: **'I am not except one of the Muslims.'"**[77]

And this has been successively narrated from the chief of the believers 'Alee ibn Abee Taalib, may Allaah be pleased with him. Rather, it has come from him that he has said:

> "No one is to show preference to me over Aboo Bakr and 'Umar lest I will lash him with the lashing of one who has slandered."[78]

This is because he has invented a lie when he gave 'Alee precedence over the two deputies. The texts which have come showing the virtue of Aboo Bakr and 'Umar over the rest are very many. The people of knowledge have cited them within the books which mention the virtues of the companions; and the preference of Aboo Bakr and 'Umar over all of the companion is a point of agreement amongst the people of knowledge.

Al-Qaadhee Aboo Ya'laa has mentioned on the authority of Imaam Ahmad that he said:

> "He who gives precedence to 'Alee over Aboo Bakr and 'Umar or prefers him over one of them

---

[77] Reported by Al-Bukhaaree no. 3671.

[78] Reported by Ibn Abee 'Aaasim within As-Sunnah no. 1219.

> in virtue without lineage, then he is a Raafidee, an innovator, and an evil doer."

The poet said: *"...then 'Uthmaan,"* meaning; then after these two deputies comes 'Uthmaan ibn 'Affaan, may Allaah be pleased with him; the possessor of two lights; the third of the rightly guided Khulafaa; the man of many virtues and praiseworthy qualities.

The poet said: *"...according to the most correct position;"* Here the word أَرْجَحْ denotes preference. It means that that which is more preponderant in the scale. Therefore, Uthmaan, may Allaah be pleased with him was the third of them in virtue based upon that which is the stronger point of view. It is as if the poet is indicating that the difference of opinion that has occurred amongst the Salaf in their statements in this regard are three. Shaykh Al-Islaam mentioned them wherein he said:

> "From them there are those who give preference to Uthmaan and it is the statement of the majority of the Imaams of the Salaf. From them, there are those who give preference to Alee, and from them there are those who withhold from speaking regarding the issue. That which Ahlus-Sunnah affirms is that the order of their virtue is similar to the order of their Caliphates."

The poet, may Allaah have mercy upon him, said:

"...and the fourth of them was the best of creation after them; Alee, the companion of goodness through goodness he was successful."

Meaning, the fourth of the companions in virtue is Alee ibn Abee Taalib, may Allaah be pleased with him.

His statement: *"...the best of creation,"* Meaning the best of the people after Aboo Bakr, 'Umar and 'Uthmaan; and the term: "Al-Bariyyah" is derived from the phrase Baraa Allaah Al-Khaaliq (Allaah brought the creation into existence) meaning that He created them. 'Alee is the paternal cousin of the Messenger of Allaah (صَلَّى ٱللَّهُ عَلَيْهِ وَسَلَّمَ) and the husband of his daughter. He is the father of the two grandsons; the man of many virtues. The poet is indicating some of his virtues in this line.

The poet said: *"Companion of goodness,"* meaning; he was a man of good and his good was perpetual. He had a large portion of goodness and attained good and acquired it. Meaning, he was always clinging to goodness.

The poet said: *"...through goodness he was successful."* This is derived from the word *An-Najaah* (success), and it is the attainment of that which one seeks and being successful in it.

In some of the manuscripts it reads بالخير يمنح (and he was granted good)" in yet another manuscript it reads بالخير ممنح (one who grants goodness) Meaning, he gives to the people and he bestows favors upon them. Within this, there is the description of generosity, goodness and nobility.

The poet said:

"Those are the people whom we have no doubt concerning upon the great camels of Firdaws shining brightly and roaming about."

Meaning; these who were mentioned from amongst the companions are the four rightly guided Khulafaa. Similarly, those who their names come within the following lines of poetry. And as for the statement of the poet when he said: *"Indeed those are the people..."* and this consists of ten men. The term للرَّهْطُ is applied to a group which is less than ten. And it is also said that it is between three and ten. Within some of manuscripts it reads والرَّهْطُ and perhaps this closer to that which is correct. The pronoun within his statement وإنَّهمُ (and indeed they) returns to the four and والرَّهْطُ (the group) is connected to them. The intent by them is the six who are mentioned within the line of poetry that comes after.

The poet said: "*...concerning which there is no doubt,*" meaning there is no speculation and no doubt concerning them and in that which they will attain from their Lord of bounty; and there is no doubt regarding their status according to Ahlus-Sunnah. There is no doubt that they are from the people of paradise.

The poet said: عَلَى نُجُبِ (upon nujub) This is the plural of *Najeeb,* and it refers to the choicest of wealth and the best of it. What is intended is they will be roaming about in Al-Firdaws upon *Nujub,* and this refers to the noble camels and noble steeds which they will travel upon and spend their days within paradise.

Muslim reported on the authority of Aboo Mas'ud Al-Ansaree that he said:

> "A man came with a she-camel and said: 'This she-camel I'm giving in the path of Allaah.' The Messenger of Allaah (ﷺ) said:

لَكَ بِهَا يَوْمَ الْقِيَامَةِ سَبْعَمِائَة نَاقَةً كُلُّهَا مَخْطُومَةٌ

"By way of it you shall have on the day of judgment seven-hundred she-camels, all being marked."[79]

It is reported by At-Tirmidhee on the authority of Sulaymaan ibn Buraydah ibn Al-Haseeb from his father that a man asked the Prophet (ﷺ) saying:

"O Messenger of Allaah, will there be horses in paradise?" The Prophet (ﷺ) said:

إِنَّ اللهَ أَدْخَلَكَ الْجَنَّةَ فَلَا تَشَاءُ أَنْ تَحْمِلَ فِيهَا عَلَى فَرَسٍ مِنْ يَاقُوتَةٍ حَمْرَاءَ يَطِيرُ بِكَ فِي الْجَنَّةِ حَيْثُ شِئْتَ إِلَّا فَعَلْتَ

"If Allaah causes you to enter into paradise then you will not wish to be carried therein upon a horse made of red rubies which will fly with you within paradise where you will except that this will happen."

And a man asked him saying: "O Messenger of Allaah will there be camels in paradise?" He said: "And he did not say to him the likes of that which he said to his companion. Rather he said:

---

[79] Reported by Muslim no. 1792.

إِنْ يُدْخِلْكَ اللهُ الْجَنَّةَ يَكُنْ لَكَ فِيهَا مَا اشْتَهَتْ نَفْسُكَ وَ لَذَّتْ عَيْنُكَ

'If Allaah enters you into paradise then there shall be for you therein whatever your soul desires and whatever delights your eye.'"[80]

The chain of narration is weak. However, it has come by way of another Mursal route of transmission with an authentic chain and it has a supporting witness from the Hadeeth of Buraydah, may Allaah be pleased with him. Therefore, it is connected to that, and it is raised to the level of Hasan. Similarly, it is found within As-Silsilah As-Saheehah by Al-Albaanee, may Allaah have mercy upon him; no. 3001.

The poet, may Allaah have mercy upon him, intends by way of this that these are guaranteed paradise. The Messenger of Allaah (ﷺ) has attested to this for them. There shall come if Allaah wills, mention of some of the Ahaadeeth, which indicate that.

The poet said: *"Al-Firdaws,"* This is a name from the names of paradise and it is the name of the highest and middle most part in paradise. Within the Hadeeth

---

[80] Reported by At-Tirmidhee no. 2543.

on authority of Aboo Hurayrah, may Allaah be pleased with him, it reads; that the Prophet (ﷺ) said:

إِنَّ فِي الْجَنَّةِ مِائَةُ دَرَجَةً أَعَدَّهَا اللهُ لِلْمُجَاهِدِينَ فِي سَبِيلِ اللهِ مَا بَيْنَ الدَّرَجَتَيْنِ كَمَا بَيْنَ السَّمَاءِ وَ الْأَرْضِ ۚ فَإِذَا سَأَلْتُمُ اللهَ فَاسْأَلُوهُ الْفِرْدَوْسَ فَإِنَّهُ أَوْسَط الْجَنَّةِ وَ أَعْلَى الْجَنَّةِ أَرَاهُ فَوْقَهُ عَرْش الرَّحْمَنِ وَ مِنْهُ تُفَجِّرُ أَنْهَارُ الْجَنَّةِ

"Indeed paradise has one-hundred levels which Allaah has prepared for those who fight in His cause. Between each level is the distance of that which is between the heavens and the earth. So if you ask Allaah, then ask Him for Al-Firdaws for indeed it is the middle most and highest part of paradise above which is the throne of Ar-Rahman and from it the rivers of paradise gush forth."[81]

The poet said:

"With those who are upon them from the people of light illumination and delight and beauty."

---

[81] Reported by Al-Bukhaaree no. 6987.

His statement: *"roaming about"* means; wherever the rider wills they go. In some of the manuscripts it reads: *"In lights of eternity they are roaming about."* And the word *Al-Khuld* (eternity) refers to paradise because it is the abode of permanent bliss which does not change nor is it removed. In this lies the fact the people of paradise will visit one another therein; they will travel about and go to and fro in order to complete their delight and perfect their happiness and joy. We ask Allaah, the Most Generous, to bestow us from His bounty.

Then the poet said:

"Sa'eed Sa'd, ibn 'Awf, Talhah, 'Aamir of Fihr and Zubayr, the praise worthy."

This is explanation and clarification of the group by way of mentioning their names and these six along with the four Khulafaa constitute the ten who have been given the glad tidings of paradise. As the Prophet, (صَلَّى ٱللَّهُ عَلَيْهِ وَسَلَّمَ) has given them glad tidings of that within the Hadeeth which is authentically affirmed. So they are the group in who there is no doubt regarding their entrance into paradise. There is no doubt that they are upon the highest level of Firdaws in the gardens of delight roaming about.

There has come, as it relates to their glad tiding with paradise, numerous narrations. From them is that which is reported by At-Tirmidhee on the authority of Abdur-Rahman ibn 'Awf, may Allaah be pleased with him, from the Prophet (ﷺ) that he said:

أبو بكر في الجنة وعمر في الجنة ، وعثمان في الجنة وعلي في الجنة وطلحة في الجنة والزبير في الجنة وعبد الرحمن بن عوف في الجنة وسعد في الجنة وسعيد في الجنة وأبو عبيدة بن الجراح في الجنة

"Aboo Bakr is in paradise, 'Umar is in paradise, 'Uthmaan is in paradise, 'Alee is in paradise, Talhah is in paradise, Az-Zubayr is in paradise, 'Abdur-Rahman ibn 'Awf is in paradise, Sa'd is in paradise, Sa'eed is in paradise and Aboo 'Ubaidah ibn Al-Jarrah is in paradise."[82]

Within Tirmidhee and ibn Maajah on the authority of Sa'eed ibn Zayd there has come a Hadeeth similar.[83]

One of the poets has mentioned all of them within two lines of poetry, he said:

---

[82] Reported by At-Tirmidhee no. 3747 and it is has been declared Saheeh by Al-Albaanee within Saheeh Al-Jaami' no. 50

[83] At-Tirmidhee no. 3748 and ibn Maajah no. 133

Mustafa has the best companionship; it has been textualized that they are

In paradise of eternity and this has increased them in nobility;

They are Talhah, ibn 'Awf, Az-Zubayr, along with

Aboo 'Ubaidah, the two Sa'ds, and the Khulafaa.

The poet said: "Sa'eed" this is Ibn Zayd ibn 'Amr ibn Nufayl, who was the cousin of the chief of the believers, 'Umar ibn Al-Khattaab, may Allaah be pleased with him. And Sa'd is ibn Aboo Waqqaas, and Ibn 'Awf refers to Abdur-Rahman. Talhah is ibn 'Ubaydullaah, 'Aamir of Fihr is Aboo 'Ubaydah 'Aamir ibn Al-Jarrah Al-Firhee Al-Qurashee. Az-Zubayr refers to ibn Al-'Awwaam, Al-Mumaddah means that he is the one who has numerous accolades, and in fact all of them have numerous accolades. And from the greatest of these accolades is them been given the glad tidings of paradise.

A study has been done regarding the virtues of these particular companions within the book Ar-Riyadh An-Nudhrah fee Manaaqib Al-'Ashrah by Al-Muhibb At-Tabaree.

The poet said:

"And speak with the best terms regarding all of the companions and do not be one who speaks ill of them pointing out their faults criticizing."

Once the poet had mentioned this group, he spoke regarding the companions in general; he said: *"And speak with the best terms regarding all of the companions."* Meaning; do not let your statement of good and your excellent speech specifically be for these who have been mentioned, rather speak good regarding all of the companions; for all of them are upright and are a people of virtue and excellence.

The companion is one who met the Prophet (ﷺ), believed in him, and died upon that. Therefore, anyone who fits this description then he is from the companions. Therefore, say good regarding them. When Allaah mentioned within His Soorah Al-Hashr, the Muhajiroon and the Ansaar, He said:

﴿ وَٱلَّذِينَ جَآءُو مِنۢ بَعۡدِهِمۡ يَقُولُونَ رَبَّنَا ٱغۡفِرۡ لَنَا وَلِإِخۡوَٰنِنَا ٱلَّذِينَ سَبَقُونَا بِٱلۡإِيمَٰنِ وَلَا تَجۡعَلۡ فِي قُلُوبِنَا غِلّٗا لِّلَّذِينَ ءَامَنُواْ رَبَّنَآ إِنَّكَ رَءُوفٞ رَّحِيمٌ ١٠ ﴾

And those who came after them say: "Our Lord! Forgive us and our brethren who have

> **preceded us in Faith, and put not in our hearts any hatred against those who have believed. Our Lord! You are indeed full of kindness, Most Merciful.** [84]

Therefore, Allaah mentioned for those who come after them two qualities; they are: Firstly: Security of that which is within the breast. Secondly: Security of that which is upon the tongue. This is how the person of the Sunnah must be as it relates to the companions. Therefore, he should not harbor within his heart any rancor towards them, and his tongue should be safe. Hence, he does not criticize them nor discuss that which occurred between them. Rather, he says concerning them that which will increase love of them within the hearts.

The poet, may Allaah have mercy upon him, indicates the actualization of these two descriptions with his statement: *"And speak with the best terms..."*

There has previously been mentioned that if the word Al-Qawl (statement) is used, then it encompasses the statement of the heart and the statement of the tongue, therefore, the meaning is:

---

[84] Soorah Al-Hashr (59:10)

Say regarding them the best statement with your heart that should be free from rancor and enmity and do not carry regarding them except good; and with your tongue such that it should be free from revilement and criticism and do not speak regarding them except with that which is good.

The poet said:

"And do not be one who speaks ill of them pointing out their faults and criticizing."

Once he had ordered and encouraged the person of the Sunnah to say regarding the companions the best statement, he warned him against falling into revilement and criticism for anyone of them.

He said: طَعَّاناً meaning; one who frequently reviles them. What is intended is a prohibition of reviling the companions. It is not intended that it be a prohibition of exaggeration in revilement. At times a word comes upon the scale of فَعَّال. However it is not intended to be intensive; such as the statement of Allaah, the Exalted:

﴿وَمَا رَبُّكَ بِظَلَّـٰمٍ لِّلْعَبِيدِ ﴿٤٦﴾﴾

And your Lord is not at all unjust to (His) slaves. [85]

The meaning is that Allaah is not one who oppresses. Within a Hadeeth on the authority of ibn Mas'ood, may Allaah be pleased with him, it is mentioned:

لَيْسَ الْمُؤْمِنُ بِالطَّعَّانِ وَ لَا اللَّعَّان وَ لَا الْفَاحِش وَ لَا الْبَذِيء

> **"The believer is not At-Ta'aan (one who reviles) nor is he a La'aan (one who curses) nor is he a Faahish (one who is lewd) nor is he a Badhee' (one who has despicable behavior)"** [86]

Meaning he is not one who has despicable behavior using revilement nor is he one who has despicable behavior using foul language; and this is as it relates to the Muslims in general, so how about the affairs as it relates to the companions who are all upright?

The poet, may Allaah have mercy upon him, said: *"And criticizes." Al-Jarh* is speech, therefore delving deep into that which occurred between the companions and

---

[85] Soorah Fussilat (41:46)

[86] Reported by Ahmad within Al-Musnad no. 3839. Al-Albaanee declared it to be Saheeh within As-Silsilah As-Saheehah no. 320.

that which emanated from them is not the etiquette of Ahlus-Sunnah nor is it from their methodology. Rather, it is the state of the people of desires and a path of the people of misguidance. Here the poet affirms the trustworthiness of the companions and their status. Those who Allaah has ennobled with companionship of His Prophet (صَلَّى ٱللَّٰهُ عَلَيْهِ وَسَلَّمَ) and hearing the revelation directly from him as it was being sent down. So they are upright and trustworthy. And they are the carriers of the religion and its transmitters to the Ummah.

Ibn Mas'ood, may Allaah be pleased with him, said:

> "He who wishes to follow anyone then let him follow the companions of the Messenger of Allaah (صَلَّى ٱللَّٰهُ عَلَيْهِ وَسَلَّمَ) for they were the most righteous of this Ummah in heart and the most profound of them in knowledge, and the least of them in sins and the firmest of them in guidance and the best of them in state. Allaah chose them to accompany His Prophet (صَلَّى ٱللَّٰهُ عَلَيْهِ وَسَلَّمَ) and to establish His religion. Therefore, recognize their virtue and follow in their footsteps; for they were upon upright guidance."

From this, it is known that any revilement of the companions is no more than revilement of the religion.

This is because revilement of the one who transmitted it is to revile that which has been transmitted. For the companions are those who have transmitted the religion. Due to this, there is not a Hadeeth, which we narrate from the Prophet (ﷺ) except that the medium between us and him was one of the companions. Therefore, revilement of them is revilement of the religion. Due to this, Aboo Zur'ah Ar-Raazee, may Allaah have mercy upon him said:

> "If you see a man belittling anyone of the companions of the Messenger of Allaah (ﷺ) then know that he is a Zindeeq because the religion is the truth; the Qur'aan is the truth, and this has only been narrated to us by way of the companions. So therefore, these people desire to criticize our witnesses in order to falsify the Book and the Sunnah and they are more worthy of being criticized and they are heretics."

Hence to declare the companions to be disbelievers and to belie them is filth from the filth of the Jews. The intent of it is not merely to revile the companions themselves. The intent is to place a barrier between the people and the religion.

When the Raafidah accuse Aboo Hurayrah of being a liar or other than him from the companions, then they only launch these claims upon them in order to divert the people from the religion, and in order that they will not trust in him nor be at ease with that which he has transmitted. For indeed reviling the transmitter is revilement of that which has been transmitted. Therefore, whoever remains and he is considered to be trustworthy in the religion, and then they accuse him with lying, and they accuse him with disbelief. By way of this the intent of the people is known.

The Prophet (ﷺ) warned against reviling the companions with the sternest warning, and he commanded to withhold from criticizing them or reviling them.

Within the two Saheehs there has come on the authority of Aboo Sa'eed Al-Khudree, may Allaah be pleased with him, that the Prophet (ﷺ) said:

لَا تَسَبُّوا أَصْحَابِي فَوَ الَّذِي نَفْسِي بِيَدِهِ لَوْ أَنَّ أَحَدَكُمْ أَنْفَقَ مِثْلَ أُحُد ذَهَبًا مَا أَدْرَكَ مدَّ أَحَدِهِمْ وَ لَا نَصِيفَهُ

> **"Do not revile my companions, for by He in whose hands is my soul if one of you were to spend equal to mount Uhud in gold (as charity) that will not equal a handful spent by one of them not even half of that."**[87]

It is affirmed from him (ﷺ) in that which Ibn Mas'ood, may Allaah be pleased with him, reported that he said:

إِذَا ذُكِرَ أَصْحَابِي فَأَمْسِكُوا

> **"When one of my companions are mentioned withhold."**[88]

What is intended is that when they are mentioned with other than that which is good.

The companions, may Allaah be pleased with them are not to be mentioned except with good and with beautiful words and excellence; whilst supplicating for them to have forgiveness, mercy, and the pleasure of Allaah. This is as opposed to that which the people of filthy hearts and vile intellects do from discussing the companions or some of them in a reviling manner,

---

[87] Reported by Al-Bukhaaree no. 3673 and Muslim no. 2541.

[88] Reported by At-Tabaree within Al-Kabeer no. 1448. Al-Albaanee declared it to be Saheeh within As-Silsilah As-Saheehah no. 34.

abusing them and criticizing them. Therefore, they do the opposite of that which they have been commanded with, and they act contrarily to that which they have been called to.

Muslim reported within his Saheeh on the authority of 'Aa'ishah, may Allaah be pleased with her, that she said to 'Urwah ibn Az-Zubayr:

> "O son of my brother, they have been commanded to seek forgiveness for the companions of the Prophet (صَلَّى ٱللَّهُ عَلَيْهِ وَسَلَّمَ) yet they revile them."[89]

We seek refuge with Allaah from deviation and slander and we ask Him, Glorified be He, to not place within our hearts ranker for anyone of the people of Eemaan; and that He forgive the righteous, upright, and excellent companions and all those who follow them with goodness and excellence.

Then once the poet, may Allaah have mercy upon him, clarified the status of the companions and encouraged towards speaking regarding them with the best terms and warned against reviling them, he said—establishing the evidence for that which he has mentioned:

---

[89] Reported by Muslim no. 3022.

"The clear revelation has spoken of their excellence and in Soorah Al-Fat'h are verses regarding the companions praising them."

That which has preceded is an affirmation of that creed of Ahlus-Sunnah regarding the companions, and this line of poetry contains evidence for that creed. Due to this, the poem although it is concise, the points of study are mentioned therein along with their evidences.

The statement of the poet when he said: *"Has spoken..."* is derived from the statement of Allaah, the Exalted:

﴿ هَٰذَا كِتَٰبُنَا يَنطِقُ عَلَيْكُم بِٱلْحَقِّ ۚ إِنَّا كُنَّا نَسْتَنسِخُ مَا كُنتُمْ تَعْمَلُونَ ﴿٢٩﴾ ﴾

This Our Record speaks about you with truth. Verily, We were recording what you used to do [90]

The statement of the poet wherein he said: *"The revelation,"* refers to the Noble Qur'aan, the speech of Allaah. It is that which falsehood cannot come to it neither from before it nor from behind it. It is revelation from the All Wise the Praiseworthy.

[90] Soorah Al-Jathiyah (45:29)

The poet said: *"...clear,"* meaning it is clear and evident that which contains neither ambiguity nor murkiness. It is that which clarifies the legislations and the rulings. It makes evident that path of truth and guidance from falsehood and misguidance.

The poet said: "بِفَضْلِهِمْ (with their virtue)" this is a preposition along with the prepositional clause in connection to the action of speech. The Qur'aan is filled with evidences which clarify the virtue of the companions. From that is that which the poet, may Allaah have mercy upon him, indicated within his statement: *"...and in Soorah Al-Fat'h are verses about the companions praising them."*

In another manuscript of the poem it reads: *"Regarding the companions praising them,"* This indicates that the revelation is filled with evidences that indicate the virtue of the companions and at the same time draw attention to the numerous evidences within Soorah Al-Fat'h which praise the companions and clarify their virtues. When reflecting upon this Soorah, we find many places which contain praise of the companions. At the beginning of the Soorah Allaah said:

﴿ هُوَ ٱلَّذِىٓ أَنزَلَ ٱلسَّكِينَةَ فِى قُلُوبِ ٱلْمُؤْمِنِينَ لِيَزْدَادُوٓا۟ إِيمَٰنًا مَّعَ إِيمَٰنِهِمْ ۗ وَلِلَّهِ جُنُودُ ٱلسَّمَٰوَٰتِ وَٱلْأَرْضِ ۚ وَكَانَ ٱللَّهُ عَلِيمًا حَكِيمًا ﴿٤﴾ ﴾

He it is Who sent down As-Sakinah (calmness and tranquility) into the hearts of the believers, that they may grow more in Faith along with their (present) Faith. And to Allaah belong the hosts of the heavens and the earth, and Allaah is Ever All-Knower, All-Wise. [91]

Then thereafter Allaah said:

﴿ إِنَّ ٱلَّذِينَ يُبَايِعُونَكَ إِنَّمَا يُبَايِعُونَ ٱللَّهَ يَدُ ٱللَّهِ فَوْقَ أَيْدِيهِمْ ۚ فَمَن نَّكَثَ فَإِنَّمَا يَنكُثُ عَلَىٰ نَفْسِهِۦ ۖ وَمَنْ أَوْفَىٰ بِمَا عَٰهَدَ عَلَيْهُ ٱللَّهَ فَسَيُؤْتِيهِ أَجْرًا عَظِيمًا ﴿١٠﴾ ﴾

Verily, those who give Bai'â (pledge) to you (O Muhammad ﷺ) they are giving Bai'â (pledge) to Allaah. The Hand of Allaah is over their hands. Then whosoever breaks his pledge, breaks only to his own harm, and whosoever fulfills what he has covenanted

---

[91] Soorah Al-Fat'h (48:4)

with Allaah, He will bestow on him a great reward. [92]

Then he mentioned the state of those who stayed behind from the 'Arabs when he said:

﴿ ۞ لَّقَدْ رَضِيَ ٱللَّهُ عَنِ ٱلْمُؤْمِنِينَ إِذْ يُبَايِعُونَكَ تَحْتَ ٱلشَّجَرَةِ فَعَلِمَ مَا فِي قُلُوبِهِمْ فَأَنزَلَ ٱلسَّكِينَةَ عَلَيْهِمْ وَأَثَٰبَهُمْ فَتْحًا قَرِيبًا ﴿١٨﴾ ﴾

Indeed, Allaah was pleased with the believers when they gave their Bai'â (pledge) to you (O Muhammad ﷺ) under the tree, He knew what was in their hearts, and He sent down As-Sakinah (calmness and tranquility) upon them, and He rewarded them with a near victory, [93]

And thereafter in a number of verses that he mentioned:

﴿ إِذْ جَعَلَ ٱلَّذِينَ كَفَرُوا۟ فِي قُلُوبِهِمُ ٱلْحَمِيَّةَ حَمِيَّةَ ٱلْجَٰهِلِيَّةِ فَأَنزَلَ ٱللَّهُ سَكِينَتَهُۥ عَلَىٰ رَسُولِهِۦ وَعَلَى ٱلْمُؤْمِنِينَ وَأَلْزَمَهُمْ كَلِمَةَ ٱلتَّقْوَىٰ وَكَانُوٓا۟ أَحَقَّ بِهَا وَأَهْلَهَا ۚ وَكَانَ ٱللَّهُ بِكُلِّ شَىْءٍ عَلِيمًا ﴿٢٦﴾ ﴾

---

92 Soorah Al-Fat'h (48:10)

93 Soorah Al-Fat'h (48:18)

When those who disbelieve had put in their hearts pride and haughtiness the pride and haughtiness of the time of ignorance, then Allaah sent down His Sakinah (calmness and tranquility) upon His Messenger (صلى الله عليه وسلم) and upon the believers, and made them stick to the word of piety (i.e. none has the right to be worshipped but Allaah), and they were well entitled to it and worthy of it. And Allaah is the All-Knower of everything. [94]

Then Allaah closed the Soorah within His statement:

﴿ مُّحَمَّدٌ رَّسُولُ ٱللَّهِ ۚ وَٱلَّذِينَ مَعَهُۥٓ أَشِدَّآءُ عَلَى ٱلْكُفَّارِ رُحَمَآءُ بَيْنَهُمْ ۖ تَرَىٰهُمْ رُكَّعًا سُجَّدًا يَبْتَغُونَ فَضْلًا مِّنَ ٱللَّهِ وَرِضْوَٰنًا ۖ سِيمَاهُمْ فِى وُجُوهِهِم مِّنْ أَثَرِ ٱلسُّجُودِ ۚ ذَٰلِكَ مَثَلُهُمْ فِى ٱلتَّوْرَىٰةِ ۚ وَمَثَلُهُمْ فِى ٱلْإِنجِيلِ كَزَرْعٍ أَخْرَجَ شَطْـَٔهُۥ فَـَٔازَرَهُۥ فَٱسْتَغْلَظَ فَٱسْتَوَىٰ عَلَىٰ سُوقِهِۦ يُعْجِبُ ٱلزُّرَّاعَ لِيَغِيظَ بِهِمُ ٱلْكُفَّارَ ۗ وَعَدَ ٱللَّهُ ٱلَّذِينَ ءَامَنُوا۟ وَعَمِلُوا۟ ٱلصَّٰلِحَٰتِ مِنْهُم مَّغْفِرَةً وَأَجْرًا عَظِيمًۢا ﴿٢٩﴾ ﴾

Muhammad, (صَلَّى ٱللَّهُ عَلَيْهِ وَسَلَّمَ) is the Messenger of Allaah, and those who are with him are severe against disbelievers and merciful among

[94] Soorah Al-Fat'h (48:26)

themselves. You see them bowing and falling down prostrate (in prayer), seeking Bounty from Allaah and (His) Good Pleasure. The mark of them (i.e. of their Faith) is on their faces (foreheads) from the traces of (their) prostration (during prayers). This is their description in the Tawrah (Torah). But their description in the Injeel (Gospel) is like a (sown) seed which sends forth its shoot, then makes it strong, it then becomes thick, and it stands straight on its stem, delighting the sowers that He may enrage the disbelievers with them. Allaah has promised those among them who believe and do righteous good deeds, forgiveness and a mighty reward (i.e. Paradise). [95]

So all of these verses speak regarding the virtue of the companions, rather the last verse in it mentions the virtues of the companions within the Qur'aan and then clarifies their virtue within the Tawrah and the Injeel by mentioning their example within the Tawrah; he said that they are:

"...severe against the disbelievers and merciful amongst themselves. You see them bowing and

[95] Soorah Al-Fath (48:29)

falling prostrate seeking the bounty of Allaah and His good pleasure. The mark of their faith is on their faces from the traces of prostration,"

Their example in the Injeel is that they were:

"...like a (sown) seed which sends forth its shoot, then makes it strong, it then becomes thick, and it stands straight on its stem, delighting the sowers that He may enrage the disbelievers with them."

Some of the Salaf, such as Imaam Maalik, used this verse to prove the disbelief of the Raafidah because Allaah said therein: "...**that He may enrage the disbelievers with them,**"

And with this the poet concluded the speech regarding the companions after having clarified their status and their virtue and warning from reviling them and criticizing them and he affirmed in a succinct manner the creed of Ahlus-Sunnah wal-Jamaa'ah regarding them.

May Allaah, the Exalted, be pleased with them and make them pleased.

EEMAAN IN THE DIVINE DECREE

(21) وبِالقَـدَرِ المقْـدُورِ أَيْقِنْ فإِنَّهُ دِعَامَةُ عقْدِ الدِّينِ والدِّينُ أفْيَـحُ

21. And regarding the pre-ordained Qadr, be convinced, since it is

The pillar that combines many affairs of the Religion, and the Religion encompasses much

Explanation

This stanza is in affirmation of the sixth pillar from the pillars of Al-Eemaan; and it is Eemaan in the divine decree as has come in the famous Hadeeth of Jibreel. He said: *"Inform me about Eemaan."* The Prophet (ﷺ) said:

أَنْ تُـؤْمِـنَ بِـاللهِ وَ مَـلَائِـكَـتِـهِ وَ كُـتُـبِـهِ وَ رُسُـلِـهِ وَ الْـيَـوْمِ الْآخِـرِ وَ الْـقَـدَرِ خَـيْـرِهِ وَ شَـرِّهِ

> **"It is that you believe in Allaah, His angels, His books, His messengers, the last day and the divine decree; its good and its evil."**

This is a portion of a long Hadeeth, which is reported by Muslim on the authority of Ibn 'Umar from his father 'Umar, may Allaah be pleased with them both. And the Hadeeth has a story as has come within Muslim. Two men came to Ibn 'Umar and said to him:

> "We have with us a people who recite the Qur'aan and they say that the affair is mere happenstance, and there is no decree." So Ibn 'Umar said: "When you meet these people then inform them that I am free of them and that they are free of me. By He whom Abdullah ibn 'Umar swears by, if one of them were to have gold equal to mount Uhud and he spent it in charity, it will not be accepted from him until he believes in Al-Qadar. Indeed, I heard my father saying: One day while we were sitting with the Messenger of Allaah (صَلَّى اللَّهُ عَلَيْهِ وَسَلَّمَ) ... (and then he mentioned the Hadeeth)'"[96]

So Eemaan in the Decree is a pillar from the pillars of Eemaan, and it is a foundational principle from the foundational principles of the religion, and it is a supporting pillar from its supporting pillars. If it is

---

[96] Reported by Muslim Hadeeth no. 1.

destroyed, then Eemaan and the religion will not remain. For the religion has many subsidiary branches, however, they stand upon the six principles, and neither of them can do without the other. And from them is Eemaan in the divine decree, and by the removal of any of them the religion is destroyed and thus will not remain.

Due to this, it has been narrated from ibn Abbaas, may Allaah be pleased with him, that he said:

> "Qadar is the supporting pillar of At-Tawheed, so he who singles out Allaah, yet he denies Al-Qadar then his denial has nullified his Tawheed."

Meaning, if he does not have Eemaan in the divine decree, then there is no Tawheed. Disbelief in the divine decree is disbelief in Allaah; as Ahmad, may Allaah have mercy upon him said:

> "Al-Qadar is the ability of Allaah."

Many clear texts have come in the Qur'aan in which there is not the slightest amount of doubt, indicating that all of the affairs are decreed. Allaah, the Exalted has said:

﴿ إِنَّا كُلَّ شَيْءٍ خَلَقْنَاهُ بِقَدَرٍ ﴿٤٩﴾ ﴾

Verily, We have created all things with Qadar [97]

And Allaah, the Exalted has said:

﴿ مَّا كَانَ عَلَى ٱلنَّبِيِّ مِنْ حَرَجٍ فِيمَا فَرَضَ ٱللَّهُ لَهُۥ سُنَّةَ ٱللَّهِ فِى ٱلَّذِينَ خَلَوْا۟ مِن قَبْلُ وَكَانَ أَمْرُ ٱللَّهِ قَدَرًا مَّقْدُورًا ﴿٣٨﴾ ﴾

There is no blame on the Prophet (ﷺ) in that which Allaah has made legal for him. That has been Allaah's Way with those who have passed away of (the Prophets of) old. And the Command of Allaah is a decree determined. [98]

And Allaah, the Exalted also said:

﴿ وَمَا تَشَآءُونَ إِلَّآ أَن يَشَآءَ ٱللَّهُ رَبُّ ٱلْعَٰلَمِينَ ﴿٢٩﴾ ﴾

And you will not, unless (it be) that Allaah wills, the Lord of all that exists. [99]

Allaah also said:

﴿ ٱلَّذِى خَلَقَ فَسَوَّىٰ ﴿٢﴾ وَٱلَّذِى قَدَّرَ فَهَدَىٰ ﴿٣﴾ ﴾

---

[97] Soorah Al-Qamar (54:49)

[98] Soorah Al-Ahzab (33:38)

[99] Soorah At-Takwir (81:29)

Who has created (everything), and then proportioned it; And Who has measured (preordainments for each and everything) [100]

And Allaah has said:

﴿ثُمَّ جِئْتَ عَلَىٰ قَدَرٍ يَـٰمُوسَىٰ ﴿٤٠﴾﴾

Then you came here according to the fixed term which I ordained (for you), O Moosaa (Moses)! [101]

Therefore everything is by way of the decree; individually as well as in terms of their attributes. So the individual creation as well as that which they have from qualities like movement, residence, speech, silence all of this is by way of the decree.

There has come on the authority of Ibn 'Abbaas, may Allaah be pleased with him, as reported by Al-Bukhaaree within Khalq Af'aal Al-Ibaad.[102] That he said:

> "Everything is by way of the decree even when you place your hand upon your cheek."

---

[100] Soorah Al-A'laa (87:2-3)

[101] Soorah Ta-Ha (20:40)

[102] No. 96

A leaf does not fall from a tree except by way of the decree, even inability and ability is by way of the decree which Allaah has ordained and decreed. As the Prophet (ﷺ) said:

كُلُّ شَيْءٍ بِقَدَرٍ حَتَّى الْعَجَزِ وَ الْكَيس

> **"Everything is by way of the decree even inability and ability."**[103]

Hence everything is by way of the divine decree and it is not possible that there be anything within the creation that Allaah did not want nor did He create; therefore the dominion belongs to Him and the creation is His creation. Eemaan in this is obligatory, and Ahlus-Sunnah are united upon it. Their creed as it relates to Eemaan in the Qadar is summarized in that the servant believes that Allaah's foreknowledge and His bringing the creation into existence as well as that which the servants do from good and evil preceded everything and that He wrote all of that within the Preserved Tablet, and that the existence of everything from that is only by way of His will. And that He, Glorified be He, the creator of everything.

---

[103] Reported by Muslim no. 2655 from the Hadeeth of 'Abdullah ibn 'Amr ibn Al-'Aas, may Allaah be pleased with him.

Based upon this, Eemaan in the Qadar is not except by way of knowing the levels of the decree and they are four levels:

The First Level: Eemaan in the All-Encompassing knowledge of Allaah, and that he fully encompasses all things by way of His knowledge and that He knows that which was; that which will be; and that which was not; if it had been how it would have been.

Allaah said:

﴿ وَلَوْ عَلِمَ ٱللَّهُ فِيهِمْ خَيْرًا لَّأَسْمَعَهُمْ ۖ وَلَوْ أَسْمَعَهُمْ لَتَوَلَّوا۟ وَّهُم مُّعْرِضُونَ ﴿٢٣﴾ ﴾

Had Allaah known of any good in them, He would indeed have made them listen, and even if He had made them listen, they would but have turned away, averse (to the truth). [104]

Allaah also said:

[104] Soorah Al-Anfal (8:23)

﴿ ٱلْحَمْدُ لِلَّهِ ٱلَّذِى لَهُۥ مَا فِى ٱلسَّمَـٰوَٰتِ وَمَا فِى ٱلْأَرْضِ وَلَهُ ٱلْحَمْدُ فِى ٱلْـَٔاخِرَةِ ۚ وَهُوَ ٱلْحَكِيمُ ٱلْخَبِيرُ ﴿١﴾ يَعْلَمُ مَا يَلِجُ فِى ٱلْأَرْضِ وَمَا يَخْرُجُ مِنْهَا وَمَا يَنزِلُ مِنَ ٱلسَّمَآءِ وَمَا يَعْرُجُ فِيهَا ۚ وَهُوَ ٱلرَّحِيمُ ٱلْغَفُورُ ﴿٢﴾ ﴾

All the praises and thanks be to Allaah, to Whom belongs all that is in the heavens and all that is in the earth. His is all the praises and thanks in the Hereafter, and He is the All Wise, the All-Aware. He knows that which goes into the earth and that which comes forth from it, and that which descend from the heaven and that which ascends to it. And He is the Most Merciful, the Oft-Forgiving. [105]

And Allaah said:

﴿ يَـٰبُنَىَّ إِنَّهَآ إِن تَكُ مِثْقَالَ حَبَّةٍ مِّنْ خَرْدَلٍ فَتَكُن فِى صَخْرَةٍ أَوْ فِى ٱلسَّمَـٰوَٰتِ أَوْ فِى ٱلْأَرْضِ يَأْتِ بِهَا ٱللَّهُ ۚ إِنَّ ٱللَّهَ لَطِيفٌ خَبِيرٌ ﴿١٦﴾ ﴾

"O my son! If it be (anything) equal to the weight of a grain of mustard seed, and though it be in a rock, or in the heavens or in the earth, Allaah will bring it forth. Verily, Allaah

[105] Soorah Saba' (34:1-2)

is Subtle (in bringing out that grain), Well-Aware (of its place). [106]

The Second Level: Eemaan in the writing and that everything is written and recorded within the Preserved Tablet. Allaah, the Exalted, said:

﴿ وَكُلُّ شَيْءٍ فَعَلُوهُ فِي ٱلزُّبُرِ ﴿٥٢﴾ وَكُلُّ صَغِيرٍ وَكَبِيرٍ مُّسْتَطَرٌ ﴿٥٣﴾ ﴾

And each and everything they have done is noted in (their) Records (of deeds). And everything, small and big is written. [107]

Allaah, the Exalted, also said:

﴿ أَلَمْ تَعْلَمْ أَنَّ ٱللَّهَ يَعْلَمُ مَا فِي ٱلسَّمَآءِ وَٱلْأَرْضِ إِنَّ ذَٰلِكَ فِي كِتَٰبٍ إِنَّ ذَٰلِكَ عَلَى ٱللَّهِ يَسِيرٌ ﴿٧٠﴾ ﴾

Know you not that Allaah knows all that is in heaven and on earth? Verily, it is (all) in the Book. Verily! That is easy for Allaah. [108]

And Allaah has said:

---

[106] Soorah Luqman (31:16)

[107] Soorah Al-Qamar (54:52-53)

[108] Soorah Al-Hajj (22:70)

﴿ مَآ أَصَابَ مِن مُّصِيبَةٍ فِى ٱلْأَرْضِ وَلَا فِىٓ أَنفُسِكُمْ إِلَّا فِى كِتَٰبٍ مِّن قَبْلِ أَن نَّبْرَأَهَآ ۚ إِنَّ ذَٰلِكَ عَلَى ٱللَّهِ يَسِيرٌ ﴿٢٢﴾ ﴾

No calamity befalls on the earth or in yourselves but is inscribed in the Book of Decrees before We bring it into existence. Verily, that is easy for Allaah. [109]

As come on the authority of 'Abdullah ibn 'Amr ibn Al-'Aas, may Allaah be pleased with him, that he said: Allaah's Messenger (ﷺ) said:

كَتَبَ اللهُ مَقَادِيرَ كُلِّ شَيءٍ قَبْلَ أَنْ يَخْلُقَ السَّمَوَاتِ وَ الأَرْضَ بِخَمْسِينَ أَلْفَ سَنَةً وَ عَرْشُهُ عَلَى الْمَاءِ

"Allaah wrote the decrees of the creation before He created the heavens and the earth by fifty-thousand years whilst His Throne was above the water." [110]

And on the authority of 'Ubaadah ibn As-Saamit it is mentioned that the Messenger of Allaah (ﷺ) said:

---

109 Soorah Al-Hadid (57:22)

110 Reported by Muslim no. 2653.

إِنَّ أَوَّلَ مَا خَلَقَ اللهُ الْقَلَمَ قَالَ لَهُ : اُكْتُبْ فَجَرَى بِتِلْكَ السَّاعَةِ بِمَا هُوَ كَائِنٌ إِلَى يَوْمِ الْقِيَامَةِ

"The first thing that Allaah created was the pen and He said to it 'write' and at that time it flowed with everything which will be up until the Day of Standing." Reported by Ahmad and At-Tirmidhee[111]

The Third Level: Eemaan in the divine will and that whatever Allaah wills is and that which He has not willed it is not.

Allaah, the Exalted, has said:

﴿وَمَا تَشَآءُونَ إِلَّآ أَن يَشَآءَ ٱللَّهُ رَبُّ ٱلْعَٰلَمِينَ ٢٩﴾

And you will not, unless (it be) that Allaah wills, the Lord of all that exists. [112]

And Allaah, the Exalted, has said:

﴿مَن ذَا ٱلَّذِى يَشْفَعُ عِندَهُۥٓ إِلَّا بِإِذْنِهِۦ﴾

[111] Ahmad reported it within the Musnad no. 23,083 and At-Tirmidhee reported it no. 2155. Al-Albaanee graded it Saheeh within Saheeh Al-Jaami' no. 2117.

[112] Soorah At-Takwir (81:29)

Who is he that can intercede with Him except with His Permission? [113]

The Messenger of Allaah (ﷺ) said in describing it to Ibn 'Abbaas, may Allaah be pleased with him:

واعلم أن الأمة لو اجتمعت على أن ينفعوك بشيء ، لم ينفعوك إلا بشيء قد كتبه الله لك ، وإن اجتمعوا على أن يضروك بشيء ، لم يضروك إلا بشيء قد كتبه الله عليك ، رفعت الأقلام وجفت الصحف

> **"Know that if the entire Ummah gathered together to bring you some benefit, they will not be able to benefit you except that which Allaah has decreed for you. And had they gathered together in order to harm you with anything they will be not be able to harm you except with that which Allaah had already written against you. The pens have been lifted and the pages have dried."**[114]

Ash-Shaafi'ee has four stanzas of poetry concerning which Ibn 'Abdul-Barr said that they are from that which is the most firmly established from him. How

---

[113] Soorah Al-Baqarah (2:255)

[114] Reported by At-Tirmidhee no. 2516. Al-Albaanee graded it Saheeh within Saheeh Al-Jam'ee no. 7957.

excellent is that which was said regarding the decree. He said:

مَا شِئْتَ كَانَ وَ إِنْ لَمْ أَشَأْ   وَ مَا شِئْتُ إِنْ لَمْ تَشَأْ لَمْ يَكُنْ

خَلَقْتَ الْعِبَادَ عَلَى مَا عَلِمْتَ   وَ فِي الْعِلْمِ يَجْرِى الْفَتَى وَ الْمسن

عَلَى ذَا مَنَنْتَ وَ هَذَا خَذَلْتَ   و هَذَا أَعَنْتَ وَ ذَا لَمْ تُعِن

فَمِنْهُمْ شَقِي وَ مِنْهُمْ سَعِيدٌ   وَ مِنْهُمْ قَبِيحٌ وَ مِنْهُمْ حَسَنٌ

"That which You will is, even if I did not will it,

And that which I will if You did not will it then it will never be;

You have created the servants upon that which You know,

And based upon knowledge, moves the youth as well as the elderly;

Upon this one You bestow blessings and this one You leave,

And this one You aid and this one You do not.

From them there is the wretched and from them there is the blessed;

From them there is the repugnant and from them there is the beautiful."

The Fourth Level: Eemaan in the bringing into existence and creation, and that the One who brings into existence; the creator of all things is Allaah, the Exalted.

As Allaah, the Exalted has said:

﴿ ٱلْحَمْدُ لِلَّهِ رَبِّ ٱلْعَٰلَمِينَ ۝٢ ﴾

All the praises and thanks be to Allaah, the Lord of all that exists. [115]

And Allaah also said:

﴿ ٱللَّهُ خَٰلِقُ كُلِّ شَىْءٍ ۖ وَهُوَ عَلَىٰ كُلِّ شَىْءٍ وَكِيلٌ ۝٦٢ ﴾

Allaah is the Creator of all things, and He is the Wakeel (Trustee, Disposer of affairs, Guardian, etc.) over all things. [116]

Allaah has also said:

﴿ وَٱللَّهُ خَلَقَكُمْ وَمَا تَعْمَلُونَ ۝٩٦ ﴾

---

[115] Soorah Al-Fatihah (1:2)

[116] Soorah Az-Zumar (39:62)

"While Allaah has created you and what you make!" [117]

So these are the levels of Al-Qadar. There is no created thing except that it operates by way of these levels and these levels are such that one cannot have Eemaan in the Qadar except by believing in them. For each level from amongst them there are tens of evidences from the book and the Sunnah. They all have been combined in one stanza of poetry wherein the poet said:

عِلْمٌ كِتَابَةُ مَوْلَانَا مَشِيئَتُهُ   وَ خَلْقُهُ وَ هُوَ إِيجَادٌ وَ تَكْوِينٌ

"Knowledge, writing, in accordance with His will,

His creation and His bringing into existence and fashioning all things."

Moreover, two groups within the Ummah went astray regarding this affair, a group whose deviation was the denial of the decree and another by way of exaggeration in affirming it. Each of them are upon two contradictory extremes and each group has blameworthy objectives, and the best of affairs are those which are in the middle.

---

[117] Soorah As-Saffat (37:96)

The extremist deniers of the decree used to deny the decree in its four levels and more than one of the people of knowledge have mentioned that they have become extinct. Then there came a succession after them who affirmed the knowledge and the writing but they rejected the will and the creation.

They say that Allaah knows the actions of the servant and wrote it, however He did not will it nor did He create it, He only created the person. Ash-Shaafi'ee, may Allaah have mercy on him, said:

> "Debate the Qadariyah regarding the knowledge and if they reject it then they have disbelieved and if they affirm it then they have contradicted themselves."

These people are called the Qadariyah negationist; they are Mu'tazilah as well. They are those who it has been narrated regarding them that they are the *Majoos* of this Ummah, due to their statement that there are two creators; similar to the *Majoos* who used to affirm two creators; one of light and the other of darkness. The Mu'tazilah affirm, likewise, two creators; Allaah who is the creator of the individuals and the human being who is the creator of his actions.

In opposition to these Qadariyah are the Mujabbirah and they are the Jabbariyah Al-Jahmiyah. They are those who have gone to extremes in affirming the Qadar. They say that the servant's actions are by Allaah's ability and not by the ability or the will of the servant. Rather, the servant is similar to a leaf blowing in the wind having no control over his own actions, and the actual doer of the action is Allaah while the person has no free will. Rather, he is like a leaf blowing in the wind. Due to this, they are called Jabbariyah. And these individuals do not agree with their own methodology in all instances. Rather, they agree with it at times and not at others; this is contradiction and contradiction is evidence for the corruption of one's methodology. This is the custom of the people of innovation; they fall into contradiction. So if the Jabbaree were to commit fornication, abandon the prayer and commit the destructive deadly sins and they were presented for judgment, then he would say: *"I am compelled, similar to a leaf blowing in the wind,"* whereas he himself if someone were to strike him or transgress against his wealth, or a right from amongst his rights and then say to him: *"I am like a leaf blowing in the wind."* He will not accept that from him, and this is contradiction. Therefore, in affairs which they like then they say: *"I am compelled."* And if someone were to do to him that which he dislikes, then they would abandon their methodology.

From this it is known that the methodology of the people of innovation is not derived from (authentic) creed, it is rather derived from desires and lusts. Due to this, some of the people of knowledge said to one of them: *"As it relates to obedience, you are a Qadaree and as it relates to disobedience, you are a Jabbaree."* because when it comes to doing obedience, he says: *"I did it by way of my own will and not by the ability of Allaah."* and if he does an act of disobedience then he says: *"I am compelled to do it and it was not by my own will."* This clarifies that they are people of desires, and those who follow their caprices. Both groups are refuted by way of the statement of Allaah, the Exalted:

﴿ لِمَن شَآءَ مِنكُمْ أَن يَسْتَقِيمَ ﴿٢٨﴾ وَمَا تَشَآءُونَ إِلَّآ أَن يَشَآءَ ٱللَّهُ رَبُّ ٱلْعَٰلَمِينَ ﴿٢٩﴾ ﴾

To whomsoever among you who wills to walk straight. And you will not, unless (it be) that Allaah wills, the Lord of all that exists. [118]

Within his statement: **"He from amongst you who wills..."** is a refutation against the Jabbariyah, and within his statement: **"But you cannot will unless be**

---

[118] Soorah At-Takwir (81:28-29)

that Allaah wills..." is a refutation against the Qadariyah.

The poet said: *"...and regarding the pre-ordained Qadar be convinced,"* Meaning believe in the pre-ordainment. i.e., That which has emanated from the Lord, Glorified be He, being decreed and adjudicated.

We have come to know that there is no Eemaan in the Qadar except by way of having Eemaan in its four levels. The statement of the poet: "أيْقِنْ (be convinced)" means: Have certainty, which is the opposite of doubt. What is intended is let there not be within your heart any doubt in this. Therefore, certainty negates doubt. And it is complete knowledge and its perfection. For if there is found doubt or hesitation or speculation (within the heart of the individual) then certainty ceases. It is not sufficient that one simply have knowledge. Rather, it is a must that one has certainty.

The poet said: *"It is the pillar that combines the affairs of the religion,"* The word *Ad-Di'aamah* is the pillar of a house and the foundation of a building. The word Al-'Iqd is a necklace. Therefore the Deen is a phrase used for a binding tie which connects many affairs; and it has various types of branches and numerous parts and an abundance of actions. It also has pillars and foundations upon which its structure stands. And

Eemaan in the Qadar is one of these pillars and foundations upon which this building stands.

This emphasizes the fact that if this pillar ceases then this leads to the ceasing of the religion and Eemaan; as well as the loss of this blessed tie. The word Deen bearing the definite article ال in this instance denotes a covenant and it is either understood or mentioned. Here it is understood, meaning that the religion which one is bound by is the religion of Al-Islaam.

Allaah says within the Qur'aan:

﴿ إِنَّ ٱلدِّينَ عِندَ ٱللَّهِ ٱلْإِسْلَٰمُ ﴾

Truly, the religion with Allaah is Al-Islaam. [119]

And it is the religion which Allaah is pleased with for His servants. Allaah has said:

﴿ ٱلْيَوْمَ أَكْمَلْتُ لَكُمْ دِينَكُمْ وَأَتْمَمْتُ عَلَيْكُمْ نِعْمَتِى وَرَضِيتُ لَكُمُ ٱلْإِسْلَٰمَ دِينًا ﴾

This day, I have perfected your religion for you, completed My Favour upon you, and have chosen for you Islaam as your religion. [120]

[119] Soorah Aali Imran (3:19)

And Allaah will not accept any religion for anyone other than it. Allaah has said:

﴿ وَمَن يَبْتَغِ غَيْرَ ٱلْإِسْلَٰمِ دِينًا فَلَن يُقْبَلَ مِنْهُ وَهُوَ فِى ٱلْءَاخِرَةِ مِنَ ٱلْخَٰسِرِينَ ﴿٨٥﴾ ﴾

And whoever seeks a religion other than Islaam, it will never be accepted of him, and in the Hereafter he will be one of the losers. [121]

The poet said: *"It encompasses much,"* meaning that it is broad and it has many actions within it, and numerous acts of obedience and various types of acts of worship and many rulings, however it stands upon firm pillars and strong foundations. And from those pillars is Eemaan in the divine decree. It is proper that it be known that Eemaan in the divine decree does not negate acting by way of the means; rather, from completion of Eemaan in the Qadar is acting with the means.

The Hadeeth of 'Alee, may Allaah be pleased with him, from the Messenger of Allaah (ﷺ) clarifies this wherein some of his companions said to him:

---

120 Soorah Al-Ma'idah (5:3)

121 Soorah Aali Imran (3:85)

"By way of what is ones actions? Is it an affair which is happenstance or is it an affair which is decreed and pre-ordained." He said:

بَـلْ فِـيـمَـا قَـدَرَ وَ قَـضَـى

"Rather it is an affair which is decreed and pre-ordained."

They said: *"So therefore why should we do actions?"* He said:

اعملوا فكل ميسر لما خلق له فمن كان من أهل السعادة فَيُسَّرُه الله لِعَمَلِ

أَهْلِ السَّعَادَةِ، وَمَنْ كَانَ مِنْ أَهْلِ الشَّقَاوة فَيَسَّره لِعَمَلِ أَهْلِ الشَّقَاوَةِ

"Do actions, for everyone will have it easy to do the actions that he has been created for. So he who is from the people of happiness, Allaah will facilitate for him the actions of the people of happiness. And he who is from the people of wretchedness, then he will facilitate for him the actions of the people of wretchedness."[122]

This statement from the Prophet (ﷺ) contains that which brings about certainty and sufficiency. Due

[122] Reported by Al-Bukhaaree no. 4948 and Muslim no. 2647.

to this, when he said that to them then there were two affairs that were found with them; the first is that they believed in Al-Qadar, and secondly they competed in doing righteous actions and striving hard in doing acts of obedience.

The statement of the Prophet (ﷺ) within the Hadeeth wherein he said: ***"Do actions..."*** is not directed to one who has no free will. Rather, it is directed to one who has a free will by way of which he chooses to do that which he wants and this indicates that the individual has free will with which he chooses that which he wants to do. And this is affirmed with every person within the affairs of the Dunyaa.

And his statement (ﷺ): ***"For everyone will find it easy to do the deeds that he has been created for."*** Meaning, that the will of the servant with which he acts is subsidiary to the will of Allaah. Therefore, the servant has free will to choose that which he wants and he is not compelled like a leaf blowing within the wind. And since the affair is like this, then it is upon us to be diligent in that which benefits us and seeks the help of Allaah and seek from Him aid and success, as the Prophet (ﷺ) said in that which is reported from him by Aboo Hurayrah, may Allaah be pleased with him:

اِحْـرِصْ عَـلَـى مَـا يَـنْـفَـعُـكَ وَاسْـتَـعِـنْ بِـاللهِ

"Be diligent upon that which benefits you and seek the help of Allaah."[123]

[123] Reported by Muslim no. 2664.

EEMAAN IN THE LAST DAY

(22) وَلا تُنْكِرَنْ جَهلاً نَكِيرًا ومُنْكَـراً وَلا الحَوْضَ والمِيزانَ إنَّـكَ تُنْصَـحُ

(23) وقُـلْ يُخْـرِجُ اللهُ العَظِيمُ بِفَضلِـهِ مِن النارِ أجْسادًا مِن الفَحْمِ تُطْرَحُ

(24) عَلَى النَّهرِ في الفِردوسِ تَحْيا بِمائِهِ كَحَبِّ حَمِيلِ السَّيْلِ إذْ جاءَ يَطْفَحُ

(25) فإنَّ رَسُـولَ اللـهِ للخَلْـقِ شَافـعٌ وقُلْ فِي عَذابِ القَبرِ حـقٌّ مُوَضَّحُ

22. And do not reject, out of ignorance, (belief in) Nakeer and Munkar,

Or the Pool or the Scales, surely you are being advised sincerely.

23. And say: Allaah, the Great, will remove, from of His Grace,

Out of the Fire, people, burned severely, who will then be tossed

24. Into the river in Firdaws, wherein they will regain life by its water,

Like a seed taken by a flood that comes and wipes things away with its abundant water.

25. And surely, the Messenger of Allaah will intercede for the creation.

And speak about the punishment of the grave, that it is the truth, made clear.

Explanation

Within these stanzas, the poet speaks regarding Eemaan in the last day, which is one of the six pillars of Eemaan. There has already preceded within the previous lines of poetry some of these pillars, and these six pillars are connected; none of them are separate from the others. Eemaan in some of them obligates Eemaan in the others; and disbelief in some of them necessitates disbelief in the others. These pillars are combined within many texts from the Qur'aan.

Allaah, the Exalted, said:

﴿ لَّيْسَ ٱلْبِرَّ أَن تُوَلُّوا۟ وُجُوهَكُمْ قِبَلَ ٱلْمَشْرِقِ وَٱلْمَغْرِبِ وَلَٰكِنَّ ٱلْبِرَّ مَنْ
ءَامَنَ بِٱللَّهِ وَٱلْيَوْمِ ٱلْءَاخِرِ وَٱلْمَلَٰٓئِكَةِ وَٱلْكِتَٰبِ وَٱلنَّبِيِّۦنَ وَءَاتَى ٱلْمَالَ
عَلَىٰ حُبِّهِۦ ذَوِى ٱلْقُرْبَىٰ وَٱلْيَتَٰمَىٰ وَٱلْمَسَٰكِينَ وَٱبْنَ ٱلسَّبِيلِ وَٱلسَّآئِلِينَ
وَفِى ٱلرِّقَابِ وَأَقَامَ ٱلصَّلَوٰةَ وَءَاتَى ٱلزَّكَوٰةَ وَٱلْمُوفُونَ بِعَهْدِهِمْ إِذَا
عَٰهَدُوا۟ ۖ وَٱلصَّٰبِرِينَ فِى ٱلْبَأْسَآءِ وَٱلضَّرَّآءِ وَحِينَ ٱلْبَأْسِ ۗ أُو۟لَٰٓئِكَ ٱلَّذِينَ صَدَقُوا۟ ۖ
وَأُو۟لَٰٓئِكَ هُمُ ٱلْمُتَّقُونَ ﴿١٧٧﴾ ﴾

It is not Al-Birr (piety, righteousness, and each and every act of obedience to Allaah, etc.) that you turn your faces towards east and (or) west (in prayers); but Al-Birr is (the quality of) the one who believes in Allaah, the Last Day, the Angels, the Book, the Prophets and gives his wealth, in spite of love for it, to the kinsfolk, to the orphans, and to the poor, and to the wayfarer, and to those who ask, and to set slaves free, establishes As-Salât, and gives the Zakat, and who fulfill their covenant when they make it, and who are patient in extreme poverty and ailment and at the time of

fighting (during the battles). Such are the people of the truth and they are the pious. [124]

Allaah, the Exalted, also said:

﴿ ءَامَنَ ٱلرَّسُولُ بِمَآ أُنزِلَ إِلَيۡهِ مِن رَّبِّهِۦ وَٱلۡمُؤۡمِنُونَۚ كُلٌّ ءَامَنَ بِٱللَّهِ وَمَلَٰٓئِكَتِهِۦ

وَكُتُبِهِۦ وَرُسُلِهِۦ لَا نُفَرِّقُ بَيۡنَ أَحَدٖ مِّن رُّسُلِهِۦۚ وَقَالُواْ سَمِعۡنَا وَأَطَعۡنَاۖ

غُفۡرَانَكَ رَبَّنَا وَإِلَيۡكَ ٱلۡمَصِيرُ ٢٨٥ ﴾

The Messenger (Muhammad) believes in what has been sent down to him from his Lord, and (so do) the believers. Each one believes in Allaah, His Angels, His Books, and His Messengers. They say, "We make no distinction between one another of His Messengers" - and they say, "We hear, and we obey. (We seek) Your Forgiveness, our Lord, and to You is the return (of all)." [125]

And Allaah said:

---

[124] Soorah Al-Baqarah (2:177)

[125] Soorah Al-Baqarah (2:285)

﴿ يَٰٓأَيُّهَا ٱلَّذِينَ ءَامَنُوٓاْ ءَامِنُواْ بِٱللَّهِ وَرَسُولِهِۦ وَٱلْكِتَٰبِ ٱلَّذِى نَزَّلَ عَلَىٰ رَسُولِهِۦ
وَٱلْكِتَٰبِ ٱلَّذِىٓ أَنزَلَ مِن قَبْلُ ۚ وَمَن يَكْفُرْ بِٱللَّهِ وَمَلَٰٓئِكَتِهِۦ وَكُتُبِهِۦ وَرُسُلِهِۦ
وَٱلْيَوْمِ ٱلْءَاخِرِ فَقَدْ ضَلَّ ضَلَٰلًۢا بَعِيدًا ﴿١٣٦﴾ ﴾

O you who believe! Believe in Allaah, and His Messenger (Muhammad ﷺ), and the Book (the Qur'aan) which He has sent down to His Messenger, and the Scripture which He sent down to those before (him), and whosoever disbelieves in Allaah, His Angels, His Books, His Messengers, and the Last Day, then indeed he has strayed far away. [126]

Therefore, Eemaan in the last day is a principle from the principles of the religion. He, who does not believe in the last day, does not believe in Allaah. The poet speaks here regarding this magnificent pillar; and because it is a summarized poem, there is no room therein to speak at length and go in depth. Therefore, he indicates some of the primary affairs which occur on the last day, drawing attention by way of that to the other affairs which it was not possible to mention, giving due consideration to conciseness in speech.

---

[126] Soorah An-Nisā (4:136)

He mentioned within these four stanzas a general mention of the affairs of the day of standing. Therefore, he mentioned Munkar and Nakeer as well as the Hawd, the Scale and the disobedient monotheist being taken out of the Hellfire, as well as the intercession and the punishment of the grave.

Eemaan in the last day has guidelines; and they are: To believe in all of that which Allaah has informed with, as well as that which His Messenger (صَلَّى ٱللَّهُ عَلَيْهِ وَسَلَّمَ) has informed with from that which occur after death. This is from the most comprehensive of that which has come in the definition of belief in the last day, due to it fully encompassing all affairs beginning from the entrance into the graves up to the people being divided into two categories; a group for paradise and a group for the blazing fire.

What enters into Eemaan in the last day as well is belief in the signs of the hour, because they are portents and indications for its nearness and the closeness of its coming.

Allaah, the Exalted, says:

﴿ فَهَلْ يَنظُرُونَ إِلَّا ٱلسَّاعَةَ أَن تَأْتِيَهُم بَغْتَةً فَقَدْ جَآءَ أَشْرَاطُهَا ﴾

Do they then await (anything) other than the Hour, that it should come upon them

suddenly? But some of its portents (indications and signs) have already come. [127]

Within the Hadeeth of Jibreel, he said to the Prophet (ﷺ) *"Inform me about the hour."* The Prophet (ﷺ) said:

مَـا الْـمَـسْـئُـولُ عَـنْـهَـا بِـأَعْـلَـمَ مِـنَ الـسَّـائِـلِ

"The one being asked concerning it knows no more than the one who is asking."

Jibreel said: *"Inform me of its portents?"* He said:

أن تلد الأمة ربتها وأن ترى الحفاة العراة العالة رعاء الشاء يتطاولون في البنيان

"That the slave lady shall give birth to her mistress and you will see the barefoot naked destitute shepherds of sheep competing in the construction of tall buildings."

Therefore the hour has major signs which indicate the nearness of its establishment and it has minor signs which come before that. Eemaan in these signs is from Eemaan in the last day.

---

127 Soorah Muhammad (47:18)

Then there is Eemaan in the grave; its trial, its punishment and its bliss and that the people will be tried within their graves. The Prophet (ﷺ) said:

عَـذَابُ الْـقَـبَـرِ حَـقٌّ

"The punishment of the grave is real."[128]

The Prophet (ﷺ) used to seek refuge from it at the end of every prayer.

The poet said: "وَلا تُنْكِرَنْ (and do not reject),"the word لا here is the لا of prohibition. And the word تُنْكِرَنْ is derived from the work Al-Inkaar; and it is to obstinately reject something and not affirm it.

The poet said: *"...out of ignorance,"* this is the reason that the action is done, meaning do not reject their existence out of your ignorance and due to the scanty amount of knowledge you have.

The poet said: "Nakeer and Munkar" these are two angels from the angels of Allaah. They have blue eyes and black faces, as has come thin At-Tirmidhee from the Hadeeth of Aboo Hurayrah, may Allaah be pleased with him, that he Prophet (ﷺ) said:

---

[128] Reported by Al-Bukhaaree no. 1372 and Muslim no. 584.

إذا قبر الميت أو قال أحدكم أتاه ملكان أسودان أزرقان يقال لأحدهما المنكر والآخر النكير فيقولان ما كنت تقول في هذا الرجل فيقول ما كان يقول هو عبد الله ورسوله أشهد أن لا إله إلا الله وأن محمدا عبده ورسوله فيقولان قد كنا نعلم أنك تقول هذا ثم يفسح له في قبره سبعون ذراعا في سبعين ثم ينور له فيه ثم يقال له نم فيقول أرجع إلى أهلي فأخبرهم فيقولان نم كنومة العروس الذي لا يوقظه إلا أحب أهله إليه حتى يبعثه الله من مضجعه ذلك وإن كان منافقا قال سمعت الناس يقولون فقلت مثله لا أدري فيقولان قد كنا نعلم أنك تقول ذلك فيقال للأرض التئمي عليه فتلتئم عليه فتختلف فيها أضلاعه فلا يزال فيها معذبا حتى يبعثه الله من مضجعه ذلك

"When the deceased is within his grave (or he said) when one of you is within his grave two angels with black faces and blue eyes come to him, one of them is called Munkar and the other is called Nakeer. They say: 'What did you use to say concerning this man?' so he says that which he used to say: 'He is the servant of Allaah and His Messenger, I bear

witness that none has the right to be worshipped except Allaah and that Muhammad is His servant and Messenger.' They will say: 'We knew that you would say this.' Then his grave will be expanded for him seventy arms lengths by seventy arms lengths and then it will be illuminated for him. Then it will be said to him: 'sleep' So he will say: 'return me to my family so that I may inform them.' they will say: 'sleep as the bride groom sleep who none is able to awaken except the most beloved of his family to him up until Allaah resurrects him from this bed of his' if he was a hypocrite, then he will say: 'I heard the people saying something so I said the likes of that which they said and I do not know.' They will say: 'we knew that you would say that' so it will be said to the earth squeeze him, so it will squeeze him until his ribs interlace and he will continuously be punished therein until Allaah resurrects him from this bed of his."[129]

The reason they are called by this name is because they come in an image which is *Munkarah* (detestable); the person is not accustomed to it and it is not

[129] Reported by At-Tirmidhee no. 1071. Al-Albaanee graded it Sahceh within Saheeh Sunan At-Tirmidhee no. 1071.

pleasing to the beholders. They are also called the two Fattaan because they put the people to trial within their graves. Therefore, Eemaan in Munkar and Nakeer is from Eemaan in the last day.

A man asked Imaam Ahmad:

> "Do we say (i.e., refer to them as) Munkar and Nakeer or the two angles?" He said: "Munkar and Nakeer, this is it."

So the Hadeeth is authentic in mentioning these two names. Therefore, it is obligatory to have Eemaan in these two names. The Mu'tazilah, who allow their intellects to rule as it relates to the legislation, reject this and they do not believe in it. They say that it is not correct that one should call some of the angels of Allaah by the names Munkar and Nakeer. Therefore they reject this by way of the intellect. This is due to overwhelming ignorance and a scanty amount of knowledge from these individuals, regarding the legislation. Due to this, the poet said: *"...out of ignorance,"* Meaning, do not reject this affair out of ignorance, O person of the Sunnah. This is an indication from him to the fact that no one rejects Munkar and Nakeer except the ignorant. As for the one who has knowledge of the Book and the Sunnah, he believes in it. As for the Mu'tazilah, although they are people of theological rhetoric, they are not from the people of knowledge.

Due to this, Aboo Yusuf said concerning them:

> "Knowledge of theological rhetoric is ignorance and ignorance of theological rhetoric is knowledge."

Therefore, knowledge is Allaah said, His Messenger (صَلَّى ٱللَّٰهُ عَلَيْهِ وَسَلَّمَ) said and the companions said. So the one who speaks with theological rhetoric even if he maybe one who is eloquent, articulate, speaks well and is able to argue his points, he is still ignorant and has no knowledge. Moreover, these two angels come to the servant in his grave and make him sit up and ask him saying:

> **"Who is your Lord, what is your religion who is your prophet?"**

Due to this, from the important affairs is spreading these three fundamental principles amongst the people and teaching them to them. This is because they are the first of that which the individual will be asked about within his grave.

For this reason, it is from the advice of the Imaam Muhammad ibn 'Abdul-Wahhaab to the Ummah that he authored his magnificent treatise *Al-Usool Ath-*

Thalaathah wa Adillatuhaa (The Three Fundamental Principles and their Evidences).

As it relates to the answer of the individual to these questions and Allaah making him firm outside of his own firmness, the people are of two categories; a category who will be punished within their graves, and a category who will experience bliss. And the punishment of the grave is true. Allaah, the Exalted, said as it relates to the people of Fir'awn:

﴿ ٱلنَّارُ يُعْرَضُونَ عَلَيْهَا غُدُوًّا وَعَشِيًّا ۖ وَيَوْمَ تَقُومُ ٱلسَّاعَةُ أَدْخِلُوٓا۟ ءَالَ فِرْعَوْنَ أَشَدَّ ٱلْعَذَابِ ﴿٤٦﴾ ﴾

The Fire; they are exposed to it, morning and afternoon, and on the Day when the Hour will be established. (It will be said): "Cause Fir'awn's (Pharaoh) people to enter the severest torment!" [130]

So they are being punished now, today up until the establishment of the hour. This is the state of everyone who disbelieves in Allaah. As for the people of Tawheed from those who were disobedient and the people of major sins, their punishment in the grave is not like the punishment of the disbeliever. They are only

---

130 Soorah Ghafir (40:46)

punished in proportion to their major sins. As for the believer, then he is given bliss within his grave.

It is not permissible to reject the punishment in the grave and its bliss by way of the intellect; by way of that which one experiences; specifically the experiences of the atheists who say that if we dig up the graves then we will not find a garden therein nor a fire and we will not see a punishment nor will we see bliss. However, Allaah, the Exalted, says in describing the pious:

﴿ ذَٰلِكَ ٱلْكِتَٰبُ لَا رَيْبَ ۛ فِيهِ ۛ هُدًى لِّلْمُتَّقِينَ ٢ ٱلَّذِينَ يُؤْمِنُونَ بِٱلْغَيْبِ وَيُقِيمُونَ ٱلصَّلَوٰةَ وَمِمَّا رَزَقْنَٰهُمْ يُنفِقُونَ ٣ ﴾

> **This is the Book (the Qur'aan), whereof there is no doubt, a guidance to those who are pious. Who believe in the Unseen and establish the prayer, and spend out of what we have provided for them.** [131]

Meaning that they believe in everything which has been hidden from them from that which the Messengers of Allaah have informed with, upon them be prayers and peace.

---

131 Soorah Al-Baqarah (2:2-3)

Then the poet began his speech regarding Eemaan in the last day by way of speaking about the two angels; Munkar and Nakeer, as well as an indication that the grave and that which it contains is the first of the stages of the hereafter. And that he who dies, then his Qiyaamah has been established. The believer believes in this and all of that which is to come thereafter. Therefore, we believe in the blowing in the trumpet, and it is the horn in which the one who has been entrusted with it; Israfeel will blow. The blowings are three; the blow of terror, the blow of swooning, and the blow of standing. Some of the scholars deem them to be two blowings. That which is correct is that they are three. Each of them has been mention within the Qur'aan. Allaah says:

﴿ وَيَوْمَ يُنفَخُ فِي ٱلصُّورِ فَفَزِعَ مَن فِي ٱلسَّمَٰوَٰتِ وَمَن فِي ٱلْأَرْضِ إِلَّا مَن شَآءَ ٱللَّهُۚ وَكُلٌّ أَتَوْهُ دَٰخِرِينَ ﴿٨٧﴾ ﴾

And (remember) the Day on which the Trumpet will be blown and all who are in the heavens and all who are on the earth, will be terrified except him whom Allaah will (exempt). And all shall come to Him humbled. [132]

---

[132] Soorah An-Naml (27:87)

Allaah also says:

﴿ وَنُفِخَ فِي ٱلصُّورِ فَصَعِقَ مَن فِي ٱلسَّمَٰوَٰتِ وَمَن فِي ٱلْأَرْضِ إِلَّا مَن شَآءَ ٱللَّهُۖ ثُمَّ نُفِخَ فِيهِ أُخْرَىٰ فَإِذَا هُمْ قِيَامٌ يَنظُرُونَ ﴿٦٨﴾ ﴾

And the Trumpet will be blown, and all who are in the heavens and all who are on the earth will swoon away, except him whom Allaah will. Then it will be blown a second time and behold, they will be standing, looking on (waiting). [133]

So the trumpet will be blown into with the first blowing and the people will be terrified, then it will be blow into again and they will fall out and die. Then it will be blown a third time and they will stand before the Lord of all that exists. Within a Hadeeth it mentions that between each blowing there is forty and it is not known forty what? (i.e. forty years, forty months or forty days).

There has come that the description of their standing is that they shall be:

---

[133] Soorah Az-Zumar (39:68)

"...standing barefoot, naked and uncircumcised"[134]

Likewise, there is Eemaan in the gathering, meaning the gathering of the people on the plains on the Day of Judgment before Allaah. All of them will be gathered; from the first to the last of them, and they will be brought together on one plateau.

Allaah says:

﴿ وَيَوْمَ نُسَيِّرُ ٱلْجِبَالَ وَتَرَى ٱلْأَرْضَ بَارِزَةً وَحَشَرْنَٰهُمْ فَلَمْ نُغَادِرْ مِنْهُمْ أَحَدًا ﴿٤٧﴾ ﴾

And (remember) the Day We shall cause the mountains to pass away (like clouds of dust), and you will see the earth as a levelled plain, and we shall gather them all together so as to leave not one of them behind. [135]

Likewise, one must have Eemaan in the sun drawing near to the people, and the people will be at variant levels of sweat. And there will be those whom Allaah shades with His shade, and those whom He will not shade.

Likewise, one must have Eemaan in the records and the coming of the Lord in order to rule and adjudicate.

---

[134] Reported by Muslim no. 2859.

[135] Soorah Al-Kahf (18:47)

As well as having Eemaan in the bridge, and all that which has come within the Book and the Sunnah.

In the poet mentioning Mukar and Nakeer and warning against rejecting their existence and rejecting that which they will establish from the command of Allaah and them being two angels from the angels of Allaah, lies an indication towards the obligation of having Eemaan in the angels in general, and likewise their names and occupations as well as their descriptions and their numbers as has come in the Book and the Sunnah; believing in that generally in that which has come in a general way and with detail as it relates to that which has been described in detail. Rather, Eemaan in them is a pillar from the pillars of Eemaan and it is a foundational principle from its magnificent principles.

The poet said:

"Or the pool, or the scales, surely you are being advised sincerely,"

Meaning do not reject out of ignorance the Hawd to which the people will come, and which Allaah has promised His Prophet and His Ummah. The description of this Hawd has come within the Sunnah as it being

"Its length is one month's journey and its width is one month's journey. Its water is sweeter than honey and more fragrant than the smell of musk. The number of its cups is the number of the stars within the sky. He who drinks from it will never be thirsty again."[136]

The Ahaadeeth dealing with the Hawd have been reported successively as had been mentioned by As-Suyootee and other than him. He mentioned that there are reported from fifty companions. There has come within the Hadeeth:

لِكُلِّ نَبِيٍّ حَوْضٌ

"Every Prophet has a Hawd."[137]

In some of the Ahaadeeth the Prophet (ﷺ) mentioned that some of the people will be driven away from this Hawd and the Prophet (ﷺ) will say:

أَصْحَابِي أَصْحَابِي

'My people, my people.'

---

[136] Reported by Al-Bukhaaree no. 6579 and Muslim no. 2292.

[137] Reported by At-Tirmidhee no. 2443. Al-Albaanee graded it Saheeh within As-Silsilah As-Saheehah no. 1589.

It will be said to him: *'You do not know what they invented after you.'"*[138]

This is interpreted to be applied to those who apostate from Islaam and died upon apostasy. From the amazing affairs is that the Raafidah interpret this Hadeeth to mean the companions of the Prophet (ﷺ) while in fact they and those who resemble them are specifically who this Hadeeth is talking about. Because the companions did not change nor did they invent anything after him, as Allaah, the Exalted has said:

﴿ مِّنَ ٱلْمُؤْمِنِينَ رِجَالٌ صَدَقُوا۟ مَا عَٰهَدُوا۟ ٱللَّهَ عَلَيْهِ ۖ فَمِنْهُم مَّن قَضَىٰ نَحْبَهُۥ وَمِنْهُم مَّن يَنتَظِرُ ۖ وَمَا بَدَّلُوا۟ تَبْدِيلًا ﴿٢٣﴾ ﴾

Among the believers are men who have been true to their covenant with Allaah; and of them some have fulfilled their obligations (i.e. have been martyred), and some of them are still waiting, but they have never changed in the least. [139]

As for those who changed and altered, they are the Raafidah; to the point that they altered the Qur'aan

---

[138] Reported by Al-Bukhaaree no. 6582 and Muslim no. 2304.
[139] Soorah Al-Ahzab (33:23)

and added to it and took away from it. So they accused the companions of that which they do. The point of reference is that Eemaan in the Hawd which has been narrated is obligatory and no one rejects it except one who is ignorant of the Hadeeth.

The poet said: *"Or the scales,"* meaning, do not deny the scales, for indeed from Eemaan in the last day is Eemaan in the scales which will be erected on the Day of Judgment. Allaah says:

﴿ وَنَضَعُ ٱلْمَوَٰزِينَ ٱلْقِسْطَ لِيَوْمِ ٱلْقِيَٰمَةِ فَلَا تُظْلَمُ نَفْسٌ شَيْـًٔا ۖ وَإِن كَانَ
مِثْقَالَ حَبَّةٍ مِّنْ خَرْدَلٍ أَتَيْنَا بِهَا ۗ وَكَفَىٰ بِنَا حَٰسِبِينَ ﴿٤٧﴾ ﴾

And We shall set up balances of justice on the Day of Resurrection, then none will be dealt with unjustly in anything. And if there be the weight of a mustard seed, We will bring it. And Sufficient are We as Reckoners. [140]

So the actions as well as the scrolls and the individuals will be weighed. So it is an actual scale which has two balances; the good deeds will be placed upon one balance and the evil deeds will be placed upon the other balance. From that is the Hadeeth of the card; the point therein is the mention of the two

140 Soorah Al-Anbiya (21:47)

balances and it is his statement: **"And a card will be placed in one balance and the scrolls will be placed upon the other balance."**

There has come within some narrations: **"It has a tongue and two balances."** It has been narrated from Ibn 'Abbaas, may Allaah be pleased with him. Aboo Shaykh reported it by way of Al-Kalbee. It is narrated as well on the authority of Al-Hasan and the mention of the tongue has not come in any Hadeeth which is Marfoo. The Ahaadeeth dealing with the scale are Mutawaatir. The Qur'aan is filled with verses mentioning the scale, and they are scales upon which the weight of atom can be weighed. Allaah has said:

﴿ فَمَن يَعْمَلْ مِثْقَالَ ذَرَّةٍ خَيْرًا يَرَهُۥ ۝٧ وَمَن يَعْمَلْ مِثْقَالَ ذَرَّةٍ شَرًّا يَرَهُۥ ۝٨ ﴾

> **So whosoever does good equal to the weight of an atom (or a small ant), shall see it. And whosoever does evil equal to the weight of an atom (or a small ant), shall see it.** [141]

What enters under this is Eemaan in the records and the taking of the records with the right hand or the left hand from behind ones back, and that which follows

[141] Soorah Az-Zalzalah (99:7-8)

this from bliss or punishment. As well as being divided into two parties; a party within paradise and a party in the blazing fire.

The poet said:

"And say; Allaah, the Magnificent, will remove from His grace out of the fire people burned severely who will then be tossed into the river in Firdaws wherein they will regain life by its water, like a seed taken by a flood, it comes and wipes things away with its abundant water."

Within these two stanzas, the poet mentions the people of major sins from the disobedient monotheist who entered the fire due to their major sins and acts of disobedience. And the fact that they will be taken out of the fire in this manner which he has mentioned, and that they shall be tossed into the rivers of paradise and thus regain life by way of its water and their health shall return to them and their shapes shall rejuvenate. He has taken this, may Allaah have mercy upon him, from the Hadeeth of Aboo Sa'eed Al-Khudree, may Allaah be pleased with him. He said: "The Messenger of Allaah (ﷺ) said:

أما أهل النار الذين هم أهلها ، فإنهم لا يموتون فيها ولا يحيون ، ولكن ناس أصابتهم النار بذنوبهم ، فأماتهم إماتة ، حتى إذا كانوا فحما ، أذن بالشفاعة ، فجيء بهم ضبائر ضبائر فبثوا على أنهار الجنة ، ثم قيل : يا أهل الجنة ، أفيضوا عليهم ، فينبتون نبات الحبة تكون في حميل السيل

'As for the people of the fire who are its people, then they shall not die therein nor shall they live, however, a people whom the fire will have touched due to their sins, they will be caused to die to the point that they become like charcoal. Then intercession will be granted to them and thus they will be brought forth in groups and spread onto the rivers of paradise, then it will be said: 'O people of paradise pour water over them.' Then they will sprout like the sprouting of a seed within the silt carried by a flood.'"

Then a man from amongst the people said: 'It was as if the Messenger of Allaah lived in a desert land.'" Reported by Muslim.[142]

His statement: *"Dabaa 'ir"* means, in groups. Within the two Saheehs it is reported from him (Aboo Sa'eed

---

[142] Muslim no. 185.

Al-Khudree) that the Messenger of Allaah (صَلَّى ٱللَّٰهُ عَلَيْهِ وَسَلَّمَ) said:

يدخل أهل الجنة الجنة وأهل النار النار ثم يقول الله تعالى أخرجوا من النار من كان في قلبه مثقال حبة من خردل من إيمان فيخرجون منها قد اسودوا فيلقون في نهر الحيا أو الحياة شك مالك فينبتون كما تنبت الحبة في جانب السيل ألم تر أنها تخرج صفراء ملتوية

"The people of paradise will enter into paradise and the people of the fire will enter into the fire, then Allaah, the Exalted, with say: 'Take out from the fire he whose heart has the equivalent to a mustard seed of Eemaan within it.' so they will take out from it those who have been blackened and they will be tossed onto the river of Al-Hayaa or Al-Hayaatu (the narrator Maalik was in doubt as to which word was used) so they will sprout just as a seed carried by the current sprouts. Do you not see that it sprouts forth being yellow and twisted."[143]

---

143 Reported by Al-Bukhaaree no. 22 and Muslim no. 184

The poet said: *"And say Allaah, the Magnificent, will remove by way of His grace,"* Meaning, He will take them out of the fire; and it is only a grace from Allaah to the point that His permission given to the interceder is a grace from Allaah and a nobility for him, meaning for the interceder.

The poet said: *"From the fire bodies from charcoal,"* because the fire will have destroyed them and caused them to die, and burned them to the point that they become charcoal, and charcoal it is a burned coal, and it is black in color.

The poet said: *"Who will then be tossed."* Meaning, they will be tossed onto the river. Therefore, the preposition and the prepositional phrase within his statement: "عَلَى النَّهرِ (onto the river) is connected to the present tense verb تُطْرَحُ (they will be tossed)

The poet said: *"Al-Firdaws"* This is a name from the names of paradise and it is also applied to the highest level of paradise. There has come within a narration that the Messenger of Allaah (ﷺ) said:

إذا سألتم الله الجنة فاسألوه الفردوس ، فإنه أعلى الجنة ، ووسط الجنة

وفوقه عرش الرحمن

"If you ask Allaah for paradise, then ask Him for Al-Firdaws for indeed it is the highest and middle most part of paradise. Above it is the throne of Ar-Rahmaan."[144]

The poet said: *"Like a seed taken by a flood,"* in some of the manuscripts it reads: "Like a seed carried by the flood." and they bear the same meaning. Al-Hibb, having a Kasrah upon the Haa is the seed of the desert which does not contain nourishment. It is also said that it is a small plant which grows inside of Al-Hasheesh. As for Al-Habbah, baring a Fat'hah upon the Haa, then it is that which the people grow and the current carries away; meaning that which the flood water carries with it. This is because when the flood comes it carries along with it seeds, then they settle upon its banks and these seeds begin to grow and are watered by way of the flood water. Thus is the state of these who will come out of the fire.

The poet said: *"When it comes and thus overflows,"* Meaning when that flood comes and it overflows; meaning that it begins to gush forth. It is said: طَفِحَ الإناء (the container overflowed) Meaning, the water within it began to rise. So these for whom this example has been struck, are the people of major sins and atrocities

[144] Its reference has preceded.

which are less than shirk. As for the polytheist disbelievers, then they will remain within the fire for all eternity. They will neither have an end put to them such that they shall die nor will their punishment be lightened therein. And they will not come out of it as Allaah, the Exalted has said:

﴿ وَالَّذِينَ كَفَرُوا لَهُمْ نَارُ جَهَنَّمَ لَا يُقْضَىٰ عَلَيْهِمْ فَيَمُوتُوا وَلَا يُخَفَّفُ عَنْهُم
مِّنْ عَذَابِهَا ۚ كَذَٰلِكَ نَجْزِي كُلَّ كَفُورٍ ﴿٣٦﴾ وَهُمْ يَصْطَرِخُونَ فِيهَا رَبَّنَا
أَخْرِجْنَا نَعْمَلْ صَالِحًا غَيْرَ الَّذِي كُنَّا نَعْمَلُ ۚ أَوَلَمْ نُعَمِّرْكُم مَّا يَتَذَكَّرُ فِيهِ
مَن تَذَكَّرَ وَجَاءَكُمُ النَّذِيرُ ۖ فَذُوقُوا فَمَا لِلظَّالِمِينَ مِن نَّصِيرٍ ﴿٣٧﴾ ﴾

But those who disbelieve, for them will be the Fire of Hell. Neither it will have a complete killing effect on them so that they die, nor shall its torment be lightened for them. Thus do We requite every disbeliever! Therein they will cry: "Our Lord! Bring us out, we shall do righteous good deeds, not (the evil deeds) that we used to do." (Allaah will reply): "Did We not give you lives long enough, so that whosoever would receive admonition, - could receive it? And the warner came to you. So taste you (the

evil of your deeds). For the wrongdoers there is no helper." [145]

This is the state of the disbelievers and their fate. As for those who committed major sins and acts of disobedience from the monotheist, their ruling according to Ahlus-Sunnah is that they are under the will of Allaah; if He wills He will punish them and if He wills He will forgive them, and if He enters them into the fire, they will not remain therein forever. Rather, they should come out by way of the intercession of the interceders and by way of the mercy of the Most Merciful of those who show mercy.

These two stanzas contain a refutation against the Khawaarij and the Mu'tazilah who say that those who commit a major sin shall remain in the fire forever. Within the two stanzas also lies an indication to paradise and its bliss and hellfire and its punishment. Eemaan in that and in all of the details of it which have come in the Book and the Sunnah in connection to paradise and the hellfire is from Eemaan in the last day.

The poet said:

---

[145] Soorah Fatir (35:36-37)

"And surely the Messenger will intercede for the creation; and say concerning the punishment in the grave that it is the truth made clear."

The statement of the poet: *"And surely the Messenger of Allaah..."* in this lies Eemaan in the Messenger (ﷺ) with all of his qualities. The Messenger is the one whom Allaah sent with a noble revelation and His wise reminder as a bringer of glad tidings or warner and a caller to Allaah by His permission and a radiant lamp. What is intended by the Messenger of Allaah here is Muhammad (ﷺ) the seal of prophets and the Imaam for the messengers and the leader of those who have white blazes upon their heads and feet.[146]

The person who has the praiseworthy station and Hawd to which the people will come, the primary interceder, may payers and peace from Allaah be upon him.

---

[146] Translators note: this is a reference to the following Hadeeth. On the authority of 'Abdullah ibn Mas'ood, may Allaah be pleased with him, who said:
"*It was said; O messenger of Allaah, how will you recognize those whom you have not seen from your Ummah?"* He said: *"From the white blazes upon their foreheads and feet; like horses with black and white traces which make them distinct from others; these are the traces of ablution."* Reported by Ibn Maajah in the book of Purification and its Sunan aspects.

The poet said: *"for the creation,"* This is an indication to the greater intercession which will take place on the plains of the Day of Judgment and which the first and last peoples envy him for. This intercession from the messenger (صَلَّىٰ اللَّهُ عَلَيْهِ وَسَلَّمَ) will be for all of the creation so that Allaah will commence the recompense.

The Hadeeth of the intercession is a Hadeeth which is successively reported. It has come by way of a number of routs of transmission from a group of companions of the Prophet (صَلَّىٰ اللَّهُ عَلَيْهِ وَسَلَّمَ) from them Aboo Bakr, Ibn 'Umar, Ibn 'Abbaas, Aboo Hurayrah, Anas, Hudhayfah and other than them, may Allaah, the Exalted by pleased with all of the companions. From these Ahaadeeth is that which the two Shaykhs have reported from the Hadeeth of Aboo Hurayrah, may Allaah be pleased with him, who said: "The Messenger of Allaah (صَلَّىٰ اللَّهُ عَلَيْهِ وَسَلَّمَ) :

أنا سيد الناس يوم القيامة ، وهل تدرون مم ذلك ؟ يجمع الله الناس الأولين والآخرين في صعيد واحد يسمعهم الداعي ، وينفذهم البصر ، وتدنو الشمس ، فيبلغ الناس من الغم والكرب ما لا يطيقون ، ولا يحتملون ، فيقول الناس بعضهم لبعض : ألا ترون ما قد بلغكم ؟ ألا تنظرون من يشفع لكم إلى ربكم ؟ فيقول الناس بعضهم لبعض : عليكم

بآدم ، فيأتون آدم ، فيقولون له : يا آدم ، أنت أبو البشر خلقك الله بيده ، ونفخ فيك من روحه ، وأمر الملائكة ، فسجدوا لك ، فاشفع لنا إلى ربك ، ألا ترى ما نحن فيه ؟ ألا ترى ما قد بلغنا ؟ فيقول لهم آدم : إن ربي قد غضب اليوم غضبا ، لم يغضب قبله مثله ، ولن يغضب بعده مثله ، وإنه قد نهاني عن الشجرة ، فعصيته ، نفسي نفسي نفسي ، اذهبوا إلى غيري ، اذهبوا إلى نوح . فيأتون نوحا ، فيقولون : يا نوح ، أنت أول الرسل إلى أهل الأرض ، وقد سماك الله عبدا شكورا ، اشفع لنا إلى ربك ، ألا ترى إلى ما نحن فيه ؟ ألا ترى ما قد بلغنا ؟ قال : فيقول : إن ربي قد غضب اليوم غضبا ، لم يغضب قبله مثله ، ولن يغضب بعده مثله ، وإنه قد كانت لي دعوة دعوتها على قومي ، نفسي نفسي نفسي ، اذهبوا إلى غيري ، اذهبوا إلى إبراهيم . فيأتون إبراهيم ، فيقولون : يا إبراهيم ، أنت نبي الله وخليله من أهل الأرض ، اشفع لنا إلى ربك ، ألا ترى ما نحن فيه ؟ ألا ترى ما قد بلغنا ؟ فيقول : إن ربي قد غضب اليوم غضبا ، لم يغضب قبله مثله ، ولن يغضب بعده مثله ، وإني قد كذبت ثلاث كذبات " ، فذكرهن أبو حيان " نفسي نفسي ، اذهبوا إلى غيري ، اذهبوا إلى موسى . فيأتون

موسى ، فيقولون : يا موسى ، أنت رسول الله ، فضلك برسالاته وبكلامه على الناس ، اشفع لنا إلى ربك ، ألا ترى إلى ما نحن فيه ؟ فيقول : إن ربي قد غضب اليوم غضبا ، لم يغضب قبله مثله ، ولن يغضب بعده مثله ، إني قد قتلت نفسا لم أؤمر بقتلها ، نفسي نفسي نفسي ، اذهبوا إلى غيري ، اذهبوا إلى عيسى . فيأتون عيسى ، فيقولون : يا عيسى ، أنت رسول الله ، وكلمته ألقاها إلى مريم ، وروح منه ، وكلمت الناس في المهد ، اشفع لنا ، ألا ترى إلى ما نحن فيه ؟ فيقول عيسى : إن ربي قد غضب اليوم غضبا ، لم يغضب قبله ، ولن يغضب بعده مثله ، ولم يذكر ذنبا ، نفسي نفسي ، اذهبوا إلى غيري ، اذهبوا إلى محمد ، فيأتون محمدا صلى الله عليه وسلم ، فيقولون : يا محمد ، أنت رسول الله ، وخاتم الأنبياء ، وقد غفر الله لك ما تقدم من ذنبك وما تأخر ، اشفع لنا إلى ربك ، ألا ترى إلى ما نحن فيه ؟ فأنطلق فآتي تحت العرش ، فأقع ساجدا لربي ، ثم يفتح الله علي من محامده ، وحسن الثناء عليه شيئا لم يفتحه على أحد قبلي ، ثم يقال : يا محمد ، ارفع رأسك ، سل تعطه ، واشفع تشفع .

فأرفع رأسي ، فأقول : أمتي يا رب ، أمتي يا رب ، أمتي يا رب ، فيقال :

يا محمد ، أدخل من أمتك من لا حساب عليه من الباب الأيمن من

أبواب الجنة ، وهم شركاء الناس فيما سوى ذلك من الأبواب ، ثم قال :

والذي نفسي بيده ، إن ما بين المصراعين من مصاريع الجنة كما بين مكة

وحمير ، أو كما بين مكة وبصرى

'I am the chief of mankind on the Day of Judgment. Do you know why that is? Allaah will gather in one plain the earlier and the latter generations on the day of resurrection, then the voice of the proclaimer will be heard by all of them, and the eyesight will penetrate through all of them and the sun will come near. People will then experience a degree of anguish, anxiety and agony which they shall not be able to bear, and they shall not be able to stand. Some people will say to others; don't you see the trouble in which you are? Don't you see what misfortune that has overtaken us? Why don't you find one who can intercede for you with your Lord? Some would say to the others: 'Go to Adam.' They will go to Adam and say: 'O Adam, you are the father of humanity, Allaah has

created you by His own Hand and has breathed into you of His spirit, and ordered the angels to prostrate before you; intercede for us with your Lord? Don't you see what trouble we are in? Don't you see what misfortune that has overtaken us?' Adam will say: 'Verily my Lord is angry to an extent to which He has never been angry before nor will He be angry thereafter. Verily He forbade me to go near that tree and I disobeyed Him, I'm concerned with myself go to someone else. Go to Nooh.' They will then go to Nooh and they will say: 'O Nooh, you are the first of the Messengers sent on the earth after Adam and Allaah named you as a grateful servant; intercede for us with your Lord. Don't' you see the trouble that we are in? Don't you see the misfortune that has overtaken us.' He will say: 'Verily my Lord is angry today as He has never been angry before and will never be angry thereafter. There has emanated a curse from me with which I cursed my people, I'm concerned only with myself, I'm concerned only with myself go to Ibraheem.' They will then go to Ibraheem and say: 'You are the messenger of Allaah and His friend amongst the

inhabitants of the earth; intercede for us with your Lord. Don't you see the trouble that we are in. Don't you see that misfortune that has overtaken us?' Ibraheem will say to them: 'Verily my Lord is angry today as He has never been and He will never be angry like this thereafter.' And Ibraheem will mention his lies and then say: 'I am concerned only with myself, I am concerned only with myself. You should go to someone else. Go to Moosaa.' They will then go to Moosaa and say: 'O Moosaa, you are Allaah's Messenger; Allaah has blessed you with messengership and speaking directly to you from amongst the people, intercede for us with your Lord. Don't you see the trouble that we are in? Don't you see the misfortune that has overtaken us?' Moosaa will say to them: 'Verily my Lord is angry today as he has never been before and will never be angry like this thereafter. I in fact killed a person who I had not been ordered to kill. I am concerned with myself, I am concerned with myself. Go to someone else. Go to 'Eesaa.' They will then go to 'Eesaa and say: 'O 'Eesaa, you are the Messenger of Allaah and you spoke to the people in the cradle, you are His word which He sent down upon Maryam and you are the

spirit created by Him. So intercede for us with you Lord. Don't you see the trouble we are in; don't you see the misfortune that has overtaken us?' 'Eesaa will say: 'Verily my Lord is angry today as He has never been before nor shall He be angry like this thereafter.' He mentioned no sin of his. He simply said: 'I am concerned with myself, I am concerned with myself. You should go to someone else, you should go to Muhammad (صَلَّى ٱللَّٰهُ عَلَيْهِ وَسَلَّمَ).' They will then come to me and say: 'O Muhammad, you are the Messenger of Allaah and the last of the messengers. Allaah has pardoned you of all of your past and later sins, intercede for us with your Lord. Don't you see the trouble that we are in, don't you see the misfortune that has overtaken us?' I shall then set off and come below the thrown and fall down prostrating before my Lord, then Allaah will reveal to me and inspire me with some of His praises and glorifications which He had not revealed to anyone before me. He will then say: 'Muhammad, raise your head ask and it will be granted, intercede and your intercession shall be accepted.' I will then raise my head and say: 'O my Lord, my people, my people.' It will be said: 'O

> **Muhammad, bring in by the right gate of paradise those of your people who will have no account to render. They will share with the people some other door besides this door. The Prophet then said: 'My Him in whose Hands is the life of Muhammad, verily the distance between these two doors of paradise is like the distance between Makkah and Humayr or like the distance between Makkah and Busraa.'"** [147]

What enters into the generality of the statement of the poet: *"The Messenger will intercede for the creation,"* Is having Eemaan in all types of intercessions which has been specifically mentioned for the Prophet (صَلَّى اللَّهُ عَلَيْهِ وَسَلَّمَ) , such as his intercession for the people of paradise that they shall enter into paradise, and his intercession for his uncle Aboo Taalib that his punishment shall be lightened as well as his intercession for the people of major sins from those who deserve entrance into the fire that they shall not enter into it. And that those who entered into it from amongst them shall be taken out from it. This intercession is common between him as well as the other prophets, the righteous people and the angels.

The poet said:

---

[147] Reported by Al-Bukhaaree no. 4712 and Muslim no. 194.

"And say concerning the punishment of the grave that it is the truth made clear,"

Meaning believe and affirm the punishment of the grave. And the word *Al-Qabr* (grave) is singular. Its plural is *Quboor* or *Aqbar*. It is from the favor of Allaah and His blessings upon the children of Adam that He has guided them to this affair as an act of generosity and kindness. Allaah, the Exalted said:

﴿ ثُمَّ أَمَاتَهُۥ فَأَقْبَرَهُۥ ۝٢١ ﴾

Then He causes him to die, and puts him in his grave; [148]

Meaning that he made for them a grave in which his body can be buried out of generosity to him and as a favor upon him, and He did not make him from those who are simply tossed upon the face of the earth such that he decomposes and the people are harmed by him, or the wild animals, birds and scavengers should eat him.

The statement of the poet where he said: *"...made clear,"* meaning it is made clear within the Book and the Sunnah. Due to this, it is obligatory upon every Muslim to say that the punishment of the grave is true

[148] Soorah 'Abasa (80:21)

and the proofs that the punishment of the graves is true from the Book and the Sunnah are very many. Allaah, the Exalted, said concerning the people of Fir'awn:

﴿ ٱلنَّارُ يُعْرَضُونَ عَلَيْهَا غُدُوًّا وَعَشِيًّا ۖ وَيَوْمَ تَقُومُ ٱلسَّاعَةُ أَدْخِلُوٓا۟ ءَالَ فِرْعَوْنَ أَشَدَّ ٱلْعَذَابِ ﴿٤٦﴾ ﴾

The Fire; they are exposed to it, morning and afternoon, and on the Day when the Hour will be established (it will be said to the angels): "Cause Fir'awn's (Pharaoh) people to enter the severest torment!" [149]

There has come on the authority of 'Aa'ishah, may Allaah be pleased with her, that a Jewish woman entered upon her and mentioned the punishment of the grave and said: *"I seek refuge for you with Allaah from the punishment of the grave."* So 'Aa'ishah asked the Messenger of Allaah (ﷺ) about the punishment of the grave and he said:

نَعَمْ عَذَابُ الْقَبْرِ حَقٌّ

"Yes, the punishment of the grave is real."

---

[149] Soorah Ghafir (40:46)

'Aa'ishah, may Allaah be pleased with her said: *"I have not seen the Messenger of Allaah (ﷺ) after he prayed a prayer except that he would seek refuge from the punishment of the grave."* Reported by Al-Bukhaaree and in another narration by Ahmad, it reads:

أيها الناس استعيذوا بالله من عذاب القبر فإنّ عذاب القبر حق

"O people, seek refuge with Allaah from the punishment of the grave for indeed the punishment of the grave is true."[150]

There has come on the authority of Aboo Hurayrah, may Allaah be pleased with him, that he said: "Allaah's messenger (ﷺ) said:

إذا تشهد أحدكم فليستعذ بالله من أربع ، يقول : اللهم إني أعوذ بك من عذاب جهنم ، وعذاب القبر ، وشر فتنة المحيا والممات ، وشر فتنة المسيح الدجال

'When one of you makes Tashahhud, then let him seek refuge with Allaah from four; let him say: "O Allaah, I seek refuge with you

[150] Reported by Ahmad within Al-Musnad no. 25,025

from the punishment of the hellfire and from the punishment of the grave, and from the calamities of life and death, and from the evil fitnah of Al-Maseeh Ad-Dajjaal.'"[151]

[151] Reported by Muslim no. 588.

THE RULING REGARDING THE ONE WHO COMMITS A MAJOR SIN AND WARNING AGAINST THE METHODOLOGIES OF THE KHAWAARIJ AND THE MURJI'AA

(26) ولا تُكَفِّرَنَّ أهْلَ الصَّلاةِ وإِنْ عَصَوا   فكلُّهُمُ يَعْصِي وذُو العَرشِ يَصْفَحُ

(27) ولا تَعتقِدْ رَأيَ الخَوارجِ إنَّهُ   مَقَالٌ لِمَنْ يهواهُ يُرْدِي ويَفْضَحُ

(28) ولا تَكُ مُرْجِيًّا لَعُوبًا بِدِينِهِ   ألا إنَّمَا المُرْجِيُّ بالدِّينِ يَمْزَحُ

26. And do not make Takfeer of those who pray, even if they commit sins,

Since all of them commits sins, while the Owner of the Throne forgives graciously.

27. And do not hold a belief like that of the Khawaarij, for it is

A position held by only those who desire it, and it is destructive and disgraceful.

28. And do not be a Murji', one who plays games with his religion,

Surely, the Murji' is joking about the religion (i.e., not taking it seriously).

Explanation

These stanzas comprise clarification of the ruling regarding the one who commits a major sin and it is the first of the issues in which there arose differences between the sects of the Ummah. The methodologies of the Khawaarij, the Mu'tazilah and the Murji'ah sprung forth (regarding this issue). So the poet, with these lines of poetry, clarifies firstly the statement of Ahlus-Sunnah which is the statement of truth. Then he mentioned the statement of the Khawaarij, warning against them. Then he mentioned after the statement of the Murji'ah warning against them.

He began by way of the statement of truth saying:

"And do not make Takfeer of those who pray even if they commit sins,"

The statement لا here is the *Laa* of prohibition, and it means: Do not believe that the people who pray are disbelievers even if they commit sins; as has come within the Hadeeth:

من صلى صلاتنا وأكل ذبيحتنا واستقبل قبلتنا فهو المسلم ، له ما لنا وعليه ما علينا

> **"He who prays our prayer and eats our slaughters meats and faces our Qiblah, then he is a Muslim and he has from rights that which we have and due upon him is that which is due upon us."**[152]

Within his statement: *"...the people of prayer,"* is an indication to the disbelief of the one who abandons prayer, and that he who does not pray is a disbeliever and he is not Muslim. The proofs for the disbelief for the one who abandons prayer within the Book and the Sunnah are very many. Allaah, the Exalted says:

﴿فَإِن تَابُوا۟ وَأَقَامُوا۟ ٱلصَّلَوٰةَ وَءَاتَوُا۟ ٱلزَّكَوٰةَ فَإِخْوَٰنُكُمْ فِى ٱلدِّينِ ۗ﴾

[152] Reported by Al-Bukhaaree no. 391.

But if they repent, perform the prayer and give Zakat, then they are your brethren in religion.[153]

Allaah, the Exalted, also says informing regarding the people of the hellfire:

﴿مَا سَلَكَكُمْ فِي سَقَرَ ﴿٤٢﴾ قَالُوا لَمْ نَكُ مِنَ الْمُصَلِّينَ ﴿٤٣﴾﴾

"What has caused you to enter Hell?" They will say: "We were not of those who used to offer their prayers". [154]

And Muslim has reported within his Saheeh on the authority of Jaabir ibn 'Abdullah, may Allaah be pleased with him, that he said: *"The Messenger of Allaah (ﷺ) said:*

بَيْنَ الرَّجُلِ وَبَيْنَ الْكُفْرِ تَرْكُ الصَّلَاةِ

'Between a man and disbelief is the abandonment of prayer.'" [155]

---

[153] Soorah At-Tawbah (9:11)

[154] Soorah Al-Muddaththir (74:42-43)

[155] Reported by Muslim Hadeeth no. 82.

Within the Musnad and other than it on the authority of Buraydah, may Allaah be pleased with him, he said: "I heard the Messenger of Allaah saying:

الْعَهْدُ الَّذِي بَيْنَنَا وَ بَيْنَهُمُ الصَّلَاةُ فَمَنْ تَرَكَهَا فَقَدْ كَفَرَ

'The covenant which is between us and them is the prayer, he who abandons it then he has disbelieved."[156]

Also within Al-Musnad and other than it on the authority of 'Abdullah ibn 'Umar ibn 'Al-Aas, may Allaah be pleased with, from the Prophet (ﷺ) that one day he mentioned the prayer and said:

من حافظ عليها ، كانت له نورا وبرهانا ونجاة يوم القيامة ، ومن لم يحافظ عليها لم يكن له نور ولا برهان ولا نجاة ، وكان يوم القيامة مع قارون وفرعون وهامان وأبي بن خلف

'He who preserves it then he will have a light, proof, and safety on the Day of Judgment. How who does not preserve it will have no

[156] Reported by Ahmad within Al-Musnad no. 23,325 and Al-Albaanee graded it Saheeh within Saheeh Al-Jaami' no. 4143

> **light, no proof and no safety; and he will on the Day of Judgment be along with Qaroon, Fir'awn, Hammaan and Ubay ibn Khalf"**[157]

At-Tirmidhee narrated on the authority of 'Abdullah ibn Shaqeeq that he said:

> "The companions of the Messenger of Allaah (صَلَّى ٱللَّٰهُ عَلَيْهِ وَسَلَّمَ) did not view the abandonment of any action to be Kufr with the exception of the prayer."[158]

And the texts which bare this meaning are many.

The poet said: "*Even if they commit sins,*" meaning, whether they commit major sins or minor sins; it is not permissible to declare them to be disbelievers by way of that. So he, may Allaah have mercy upon him, is speaking regarding the ruling of the Muslim who prays, if he commits acts of disobedience which are less than disbelief then he is not to be declared a disbeliever nor is he to be excommunicated from the

---

[157] Reported by Ahmad within Al-Musnad no. 6576 and Shaykh 'Abdul Aziz ibn Baaz, may Allaah have mercy upon him said: "Its chain of narration is Hasan." Refer to Majmoo' Al-Fataawaa 10/278

[158] Reported by At-Tirmidhee no. 2622. Al-Albaanee graded it Saheeh within Saheeh Sunan At-Tirmidhee no. 2622.

religion. As for if he falls into disbelief or polytheism, then this is another affair. Here, the poet is speaking regarding the people who pray; if they fall into sins which are less than Shirk with Allaah, then it is not permissible to declare them to be a disbeliever by way of the consensus of Ahlus-Sunnah wal-Jamaa'ah as long as he outwardly professed his Islaam and has not committed an act of disbelief. As for if he commits an act of disbelief, then he is declared to be a disbeliever. And within most of the books of Fiqh, there is a chapter dealing with the ruling of the apostate and in it affairs are clarified which he who said them or does them, then he has disbelieved and left Al-Islaam.

Shaykh Al-Islaam, the Imaam, the Mujaddid, Muhammad ibn 'Abdul-Wahhaab, may Allaah have mercy upon him, has a treatise which is beneficial and concise and titled The Nullifiers of Al-Islaam. He mentioned therein ten affairs which by way of doing any one of them a person nullifies his Islaam. Moreover, in declaring Takfeer upon an individual it is a must that evidence be established against him; and if the evidence is established against him, then at that time the people of knowledge declare him to be a disbeliever; because they are more knowledgeable regarding the conditions of the people and those from amongst them who deserve that Takfeer should be made of them and those who do not deserve that.

As for the common folk then they are to benefit from the people of knowledge. The evidences that the people who pray are not to be declared disbelievers even if they commit sins are very many. From that is the statement of Allaah, the Exalted:

﴿ يَٰٓأَيُّهَا ٱلَّذِينَ ءَامَنُواْ تُوبُوٓاْ إِلَى ٱللَّهِ تَوۡبَةٗ نَّصُوحًا ﴾

O you who believe! Turn to Allaah with sincere repentance! [159]

The address here is for those who are obedient as well as those who are disobedient, and he calls them all by way of the description of Eemaan, and in this is evidence that the one who commits a major sin is not a disbeliever. Likewise, there is the statement of Allaah, the Exalted:

﴿ وَإِن طَآئِفَتَانِ مِنَ ٱلۡمُؤۡمِنِينَ ٱقۡتَتَلُواْ ﴾

And if two parties or groups among the believers fall to fighting, [160]

---

[159] Soorah At-Tahrim (66:8)

And fighting a believer is from the major sins; in spite of this, he referred to them as believers. This indicates that committing a major sin does not expel one from the religion. Likewise, Allaah, the Exalted, said:

﴿فَمَنْ عُفِىَ لَهُۥ مِنْ أَخِيهِ﴾

So he who is forgiven by his brother, [161]

And this was revealed regarding the state of the killer; so He referred to the killer as a brother for the heir of the one who was killed—and brotherhood here is the brotherhood of the religion. This indicates that murder and other than it from the major sins is a sin that does not take the Muslim outside of the religion.

Since the poem is summarized it is not possible to exhaustively list the evidences therein, so the poet sufficed by indicating the statement of the Prophet (صَلَّى ٱللَّهُ عَلَيْهِ وَسَلَّمَ):

كل بني آدم خطّاء وخير الخطائين التوّابون

"All of the children of Adam commit errors and the best of those who commit errors are those who repent." [162]

[160] Soorah Al-Hujurat (49:9)

[161] Soorah Al-Baqarah (2:178)

Due to this, he said: *"Since all of them commit sins,"* If declaring the people who commit sins to be disbelievers were permissible, than no one would remain upon Al-Islaam; for indeed the Prophet (ﷺ) informed within this Hadeeth to which the poet indicates, that all of the children of Adam make mistakes. And within another Hadeeth, he said:

لو لم تذنبوا لذهب الله بكم ، وجاء بقوم يذنبون ، ويستغفرون الله فيغفر لهم

> **"If you were not to commit sins then Allaah will do away with you and bring a people who would commit sins and they will seek His forgiveness and that He would forgive them."**[163]

The poet said: *"...the Possessor of the Throne forgives graciously,"* as Allaah the Exalted said:

---

162 Reported by Al-Tirmidhee no. 2499. Al-Albaanee graded it Hasan within Saheeh Sunan At-Tirmidhee no. 2499.

163 Reported by Al-Haakim within Al-Mustadrak no. 7623. Al-Albaanee graded it Saheeh within As-Silsilah As-Saheehah no. 967.

﴿ قُلْ يَٰعِبَادِيَ ٱلَّذِينَ أَسْرَفُوا۟ عَلَىٰٓ أَنفُسِهِمْ لَا تَقْنَطُوا۟ مِن رَّحْمَةِ ٱللَّهِ ۚ إِنَّ ٱللَّهَ يَغْفِرُ ٱلذُّنُوبَ جَمِيعًا ۚ إِنَّهُۥ هُوَ ٱلْغَفُورُ ٱلرَّحِيمُ ﴿٥٣﴾ ﴾

Say: "O My slaves who have transgressed against themselves (by committing evil deeds and sins)! Despair not of the Mercy of Allaah, verily Allaah forgives all sins. Truly, He is Oft-Forgiving, Most Merciful. [164]

This contains indication to the greatness of the pardon of Allaah and the beautiful manner in which He forgives and the vastness of His forgiveness and the perfection of His mercy and that He, Exalted be He, is such that no sin is too great for Him to forgive. He who repents then Allaah will accept his repentance and the good deeds wiped away the sins; and the calamities expiate sins as well, and Allaah is the owner of the magnificent bounty.

The poet said: *"...the owner of the Throne,"* Whenever the term ذو is used in describing Allaah, it is of two types; the first is an attribution of a quality to the one who is being described; as has come in the statement of Allaah, the Exalted:

[164] Soorah Az-Zumar (39:53)

﴿ تَبَٰرَكَ ٱسۡمُ رَبِّكَ ذِي ٱلۡجَلَٰلِ وَٱلۡإِكۡرَامِ ﴿٧٨﴾ ﴾

Blessed be the Name of your Lord the Owner of Majesty and Honor. [165]

Therefore, Nobility and Honor are two qualities of Allaah, the Mighty and Majestic. The second; is it is the attribution of a created thing to the one who has created it, and from it is the statement of Allaah, the Exalted:

﴿ ذُو ٱلۡعَرۡشِ ﴾

The Owner of the Throne. [166]

Therefore the Throne is a creation from the creations of Allaah and this attribution necessitates Nobility and Honor. The Throne is the greatest of the created things and it is their ceiling. It is above the created things similar to a dome, and the Throne is real (not figurative). Within the Arabic language a throne is a resting place of the king. As has come within the statement of Allaah:

---

[165] Soorah Ar-Rahman (55:78)

[166] Soorah Ghafir (40:15)

﴿ إِنِّي وَجَدتُّ ٱمۡرَأَةٗ تَمۡلِكُهُمۡ وَأُوتِيَتۡ مِن كُلِّ شَيۡءٖ وَلَهَا عَرۡشٌ عَظِيمٞ ﴿٢٣﴾ ﴾

"I found a woman ruling over them, and she has been given all things that could be possessed by any ruler of the earth, and she has a great throne. [167]

Meaning, the queen of Saba'. The Throne of Ar-Rahmaan has legs as has come in the Hadeeth:

فإذا موسى آخذ بقائمة من قوائم العرش

"Indeed Moosaa will take hold of a leg from the legs of the Throne." [168]

And it has those who will carry it and they are from the angels; they are eight in number. Allaah says:

﴿ وَٱلۡمَلَكُ عَلَىٰٓ أَرۡجَآئِهَاۚ وَيَحۡمِلُ عَرۡشَ رَبِّكَ فَوۡقَهُمۡ يَوۡمَئِذٖ ثَمَٰنِيَةٞ ﴿١٧﴾ ﴾

And the angels will be on its sides, and eight angels will, that Day, bear the Throne of your Lord above them. [169]

---

167 Soorah An-Naml (27:23)

168 Reported by Al-Bukhaaree no. 4638 and Muslim no. 2374

And there are angels who surround the Throne and the descriptions of the Throne are many. It is obligatory to have Eemaan in the existence of the Throne, and it is not permissible to delve deep into it by way of corrupt interpretations. Rather, we believe that it is an actual Throne. It is magnificent, noble and majestic. We believe in all of its qualities which have been narrated within the Qur'aan and the Sunnah. We believe that Allaah rose above it in a manner that befits His Majesty, as Allaah the Exalted said:

﴿ ٱلرَّحْمَٰنُ عَلَى ٱلْعَرْشِ ٱسْتَوَىٰ ۝٥ ﴾

The Most Beneficent (Allaah) Istawâ (rose over) the (Mighty) Throne. [170]

As for the people of theological rhetoric they do not believe in the Throne. Rather, they interpret it by way of corrupt false interpretations. Similarly they distort the meaning of Al-Istiwaa' (rising above the Throne)

Allaah, the Exalted said:

﴿ ٱلرَّحْمَٰنُ عَلَى ٱلْعَرْشِ ٱسْتَوَىٰ ۝٥ ﴾

---

[169] Soorah Al-Haqqah (69:17)

[170] Soorah Ta-Ha (20:5)

The Most Beneficent (Allaah) Istawâ (rose over) the (Mighty) Throne. [171]

There is not a single word within this verse except that these people have distorted its meaning, and they have doubts by way of which they reject the Istiwaa'. From the greatest of them is their statement that had Allaah risen above His throne this would necessitate that He is in need of the Throne, and the foundation of this doubt is their comparing the Creator to the creation and understanding the attributes which are attributed to Allaah in light of the understanding the attributes which are attributed to the creation. So they deem that when the creation rises above something, then he is in need of that thing; as Allaah the Exalted said:

﴿ وَٱلَّذِى خَلَقَ ٱلْأَزْوَٰجَ كُلَّهَا وَجَعَلَ لَكُم مِّنَ ٱلْفُلْكِ وَٱلْأَنْعَٰمِ مَا تَرْكَبُونَ ﴿١٢﴾ لِتَسْتَوُۥا۟ عَلَىٰ ظُهُورِهِۦ ﴾

And Who has created all the pairs and has appointed for you ships and cattle on which you ride, In order that you may mount firmly on their backs. [172]

---

[171] Soorah Ta-Ha (20:5)

[172] Soorah Az-Zukhruf (43:12-13)

Therefore, according to them, if the ship were to go down and those who are upon it will go down, and if the animal were to fall, then the one who is upon it will fall as well. This indicates the need that one has for the ship and the cattle and all of that upon which one rises. Then they came to statement of Allaah, the Exalted:

﴿ٱلرَّحْمَٰنُ عَلَى ٱلْعَرْشِ ٱسْتَوَىٰ ۝٥﴾

The Most Beneficent (Allaah) Istawâ (rose over) the (Mighty) Throne. [173]

And they did not understand from Al-Istiwaa' which is attributed to Allaah within this verse except the same Istiwaa' which the creation makes. And they said that affirmation of this necessitates a need for Allaah of the Throne. So based upon this doubt which is within their minds they negate the Istiwaa' of Allaah above the Throne. Thereafter, they are faced with two choices; either they say that Allaah is not above nor is He beneath nor is He within the creation nor is He outside of it. Or they will say Allaah is everywhere. Therefore, they ran from evil and then fell into evil which were greater and more severe of a calamity.

---

[173] Soorah Ta-Ha (20:5)

Returning to the issue of the one who commits a major sin; the correct statement regarding him is that he is not to be declared to be a disbeliever, nor is it to be said that he is a believer who is complete in his Eemaan. Rather, it is said that he is a believer as it relates to his Eemaan and he is a Faasiq as it relates to his major sin, or it is said that he is a believer who is deficient in his Eemaan.

Then the poet moved on to mentioning two false statements regarding this issue. He said: *"And do not hold a belief like that of the Khawaarij,"* The statement: *"...and do not hold a belief,"* means, do not believe and take as your religion *"...a belief like that of the Khawaarij,"* he referred to it as being a belief, because it is a point of view that is derived from their intellects and from their own ideologies. It is not based upon the evidence from the Book and the Sunnah. The Khawaarij were called (by) this (name) due to two affairs; the first they rebelled against the Khaleefah 'Alee ibn Aboo Taalib, may Allaah be pleased with him, and they declared him to be a disbeliever and they stood before him as enemies.

The second; is that they rebelled against the Sunnah and departed from it, whether that be as it relates to that which is connected to the rulers or as it relates to other issue. So the poet warns against the Khawaarij and the Ahaadeeth which have come warning against them are authentic. Imaam Ahmad said that they are authentic from ten perspectives, therefore he is warning against the point of view of the Khawaarij in general; and from their point of view as it relates to the one who commits a major sin specifically. For indeed their methodology as it relates to the one who commits a major sin is that by way of that he becomes a disbeliever who has exited from the religion and on the Day of Judgment he will be from those who are remain within the hell fire for all eternity.

The Mu'tazilah say a similar statement as the Khawaarij as it relates to the ruling regarding the one who commits a major sin, yet they differ with them in one thing. They agree that he has exited from the realm of Al-Eemaan and that he will remain in the hellfire for eternity on the Day of Judgment. Yet they differ with them regarding the issue of describing him as a disbeliever. So the Mu'tazilah say he is neither a believer nor is he a disbeliever. Rather, they say that he is in a place between the two places. So the reality of their statement is that he does not have any Eemaan nor has he entered into the realm of disbelief. However, in reality the two methodologies are one and the same.

The poet said: *"It is a position held only by those who desire it,"* This is a subtle expression. This is because these groups and methodologies in reality their affair is merely based upon desire and they abandon the Book and the Sunnah. Due to this, there has come within the Hadeeth:

وستفترق هذه الأمة على ثلاث وسبعين فرقة في الأهواء

> **"This Ummah will be divided into seventy-three groups based upon desires."**[174]

So one's heart becomes consumed with desires and his vision is blinded, and he is not guided to the truth nor does he look at a text or a Hadeeth. Rather, he proceeds based upon his desires, and the one who desires the statement of the Khawaarij will find nothing along with it except loss, humiliation and destruction. Due to this the poet, said: *"...and it is destructive and disgraceful."*

So the fate of the one who desires the beliefs of the Khawaarij is destruction and ignominy in the Dunyaa as well as the hereafter as well as destruction and humiliation. There is nothing greater than this

---

174 Reported by Ibn Abee 'Aasim within As-Sunnah with this wording no. 69. Al-Albaanee graded it Saheeh within his checking of the book As-Sunnah.

humiliation by way of the person declaring the Muslims to be disbelievers while leaving alone the atheists; oppressing the people of Islaam while the worshipers of idols are safe from him.

Then the poet went on to mention the statement of the Murji'ah he said: *"And do not be a Murjee,"* That which the poet described the Murji'ah with is from the greatest of that which they have been described with. For indeed the Murji'ah play games with their religion and they toy around with it. The deeper that an individual delves into Irjaa', then his toying and playing around with the religion is greater. So the extremist Murji'ah say that sins will not harm Eemaan just as acts of obedience do not benefit along with disbelief. Eemaan according to them is acknowledgement only. So what mockery and playing around with their religion is greater than this? And which opening for the door of disobedience and sins is greater than this?

It is transmitted from one of the Murji'ah that he passed by a man drinking alcohol and that man who was drunk began to curse him, so the Murjee' said: *"Is this my reward while I declare you to be a believer who is perfect in Eemaan?"* Irjaa' within the Arabic language means *At-Ta'kheer* (delay) Allaah, the Exalted said:

﴿ قَالُوٓاْ أَرۡجِهۡ وَأَخَاهُ وَأَرۡسِلۡ فِي ٱلۡمَدَآئِنِ حَٰشِرِينَ ﴿١١١﴾ ﴾

They said: "Put him and his brother off (for a time), and send callers (men) to the cities to collect, [175]

The Murji'ah are called by this name because they withhold actions from Eemaan and they say that actions are not a part of Eemaan. Moreover, the Murji'ah are divided into groups.

- A group from amongst them who say that Eemaan is merely recognition.
- A group from amongst them who says that it is merely affirmation.
- Another group from amongst them will say that is merely pronunciation upon the tongue.
- And another group from amongst them who says it is merely pronunciation upon the tongue and belief,

They vary in their levels of Irjaa' while they are in agreement that actions have nothing to do with Eemaan; and in proportion to their share of Irja'a and

---

[175] Soorah Al-A'raf (7:111)

extremism therein they deserve to be described with the description that the poet has mentioned.

The manner in which they play and make mockery of the religion in light of this creed is that if it is said to the Faasiq:

> "Your Eemaan is similar to the Eemaan of the Prophet (ﷺ)."Then will he commit himself to the religion? Or will he say: My Eemaan is perfect and complete; this is my state, my Eemaan is similar to the Eemaan of the Prophet (ﷺ) therefore, what is the need for clinging to the religion.

The result therefore would be one taking the religion as entertainment and play. The extremist from amongst the Murji'ah say just as acts of obedience do not benefit along with disbelief; similarly, sins do not harm along with Eemaan. This statement is of the utmost level of vileness and corruption and it is a path which leads to the abandonment of the prayers and the withholding of the Zakat and the abandonment of fasting, Hajj and other than this from the acts of obedience and it is a means to committing obscene actions and destructive sins.

The one who has sound intellect does not doubt that this is playing with their religion. And what form of playing with their religion is more despicable and more severe than this form of playing. At any rate, these three stanzas contain clarification of the statement of the groups regarding the one who commits the major sin and they are three statements; the statement of Ahlus-Sunnah wal-Jamaa'ah—and it is the statement which is just and balanced—and two contradictory statements.

THE DEFINITION OF EEMAAN; ITS INCREASE AND DECREASE

(29) وقُــلْ إنَّما الإيمانُ قَــوْلٌ ونيَّــةٌ وِفعْلٌ عَلَى قَــولِ النبيِّ مُصَرَّحُ

(30) ويَنْقُصُ طَـوْرًا بالمعَاصِي وَتَـارةً بطَاعَتِهِ يَنْمِي وفي الوَزنِ يَرْجَحُ

29. And say: Eemaan (faith) consists of statements, intentions (i.e. belief of the heart)

And Actions, according to the explicit statement of the Prophet.

30. And it decreases sometimes, due to disobedience, and sometimes

Because of obedience it grows, and on the Scale it will outweigh (other things).

Explanation

The poet, may Allaah have mercy upon him, mentioned within these lines of poetry the creed of

Ahlus-Sunnah as it relates to Eemaan, and that according to them it has three pillars.

1. Belief with the heart
2. Statement with the tongue
3. Action of the heart and limbs

Many evidences from the book of Allaah and the Sunnah of the Messenger of Allaah (ﷺ) prove the fact that these three affairs enter into in Al-Eemaan, such that they cannot be counted due to their abundance. The poet, may Allaah have mercy upon him, as is his way, calls the person of the Sunnah to the correct and sound creed free from filth, he says: *"And say the Eemaan consists of statements, intentions, and actions,"* So as it relates to the statements this is by way of the person saying with his tongue that which Allaah has commanded him to say and this is of two categories: The first, is the foundation; and it is statement which the religion stands upon and is predicated upon; which is the two testimonies. In the Hadeeth, the Prophet (ﷺ) said:

أُمِرْتُ أَنْ أُقَاتِلَ النَّاسَ حَتَّى يَقُولُوا لَا إِلَهَ إِلَّا اللهُ

"I have been commanded to fight the people until they say that none has the right to be worshiped except Allaah."[176]

The second; is that which is a subsidiary branch and it is that which is built upon this foundation and extends out from it; and this refers to the rest of the statements of obedience which are performed with the tongue such as; Tasbeeh (glorification of Allaah), the recitation of the Qur'aan, enjoining the good, forbidding the evil and the likes of that.

The statement of the poet wherein he said: *"...and intention,"* meaning, the correct belief within the heart upon which his actions are based. The Prophet (صَلَّى اللهُ عَلَيْهِ وَسَلَّمَ) said:

إِنَّمَا الأَعْمَالُ بِالنِّيَّاتِ

"Indeed actions are but by intentions."[177]

Therefore, when the person has statements and actions, however does not have intention within his heart then he is a hypocrite and he is one whose righteous actions are apparent however his inner

[176] Reported by Al-Bukhaaree no. 2946 and Muslim no. 21.

[177] Reported by Al-Bukhaaree no. 1 and Muslim no. 1907

condition opposes that. Allaah, the Exalted, said in clarification of the state of the hypocrites:

﴿ وَإِذَا لَقُوا۟ ٱلَّذِينَ ءَامَنُوا۟ قَالُوٓا۟ ءَامَنَّا وَإِذَا خَلَوْا۟ إِلَىٰ شَيَـٰطِينِهِمْ قَالُوٓا۟ إِنَّا مَعَكُمْ إِنَّمَا نَحْنُ مُسْتَهْزِءُونَ ﴿١٤﴾ ﴾

And when they meet those who believe, they say: "We believe," but when they are alone with their devils, they say: "Truly, we are with you; verily, we were but mocking." [178]

And Allaah also said:

﴿ إِذَا جَآءَكَ ٱلْمُنَـٰفِقُونَ قَالُوا۟ نَشْهَدُ إِنَّكَ لَرَسُولُ ٱللَّهِ ۗ وَٱللَّهُ يَعْلَمُ إِنَّكَ لَرَسُولُهُۥ وَٱللَّهُ يَشْهَدُ إِنَّ ٱلْمُنَـٰفِقِينَ لَكَـٰذِبُونَ ﴿١﴾ ﴾

When the hypocrites come to you (O Muhammad ﷺ), they say: "We bear witness that you are indeed the Messenger of Allaah." Allaah knows that you are indeed His Messenger and Allaah bears witness that the hypocrites are liars indeed. [179]

---

[178] Soorah Al-Baqarah (2:14)

[179] Soorah Al-Munafiqun (63:1)

The statement of the poet wherein he said: *"...and actions,"* meaning, actions enter into the title of Al-Eemaan, and no one says that actions are outside of Eemaan with the exception of the Murji'ah. Speech regarding them as already preceded. Actions are ones deeds, and it includes actions of the heart; such as love, fear, turning in repentance, *Al-Hayaa* (modesty), reliance, and other than these from the actions of the heart. As well as actions of the limbs; such as prayer, fasting, Zakat, Jihaad, righteousness to the parents, joining the ties of the womb, and other than this from the actions of the limbs.

From the Ahaadeeth which are comprehensive of these three affairs is the Hadeeth of Aboo Hurayrah which is known of the Hadeeth of the branches of Eemaan. The Prophet (ﷺ) said:

الإيمان بضع وسبعون شعبة فأعلاها قول لا إله إلا الله ، وأدناها إماطة

الأذى عن الطريق ، والحياء شعبة من الإيمان

> **"Eemaan is seventy some odd branches, the highest of them is the statement that 'None has the right to be worshipped except Allaah', the lowest of them is to remove something**

harmful from the road, and Al-Hayaa is a branch of Al-Eemaan."[180]

This comprehensive Hadeeth indicates that that which is upon the tongue, actions and heart all enter into the title Al-Eemaan. As for its indication of that which is upon the tongue, it is within his statement:

"The highest of them is the statement La Ilaha Illa Allaah,"

And statement includes the statement of the heart and the statement of the tongue when it is applied.

Allaah, the Exalted, said:

﴿ إِنَّ ٱلَّذِينَ قَالُواْ رَبُّنَا ٱللَّهُ ثُمَّ ٱسْتَقَٰمُواْ تَتَنَزَّلُ عَلَيْهِمُ ٱلْمَلَٰٓئِكَةُ أَلَّا تَخَافُواْ وَلَا تَحْزَنُواْ وَأَبْشِرُواْ بِٱلْجَنَّةِ ٱلَّتِى كُنتُمْ تُوعَدُونَ ﴿٣٠﴾ ﴾

Verily, those who say: "Our Lord is Allaah (Alone)," and then they are upright upon it, on them the angels will descend (saying): "Fear not, nor grieve! But receive the glad tidings of Paradise which you have been promised!" [181]

Allaah, the Exalted, also said:

---

[180] Reported by Al-Bukhaaree no. 9 and Muslim no. 35

[181] Soorah Fussilat (41:30)

﴿ قُولُوٓاْ ءَامَنَّا بِٱللَّهِ وَمَآ أُنزِلَ إِلَيۡنَا وَمَآ أُنزِلَ إِلَىٰٓ إِبۡرَٰهِـۧمَ وَإِسۡمَٰعِيلَ وَإِسۡحَٰقَ وَيَعۡقُوبَ وَٱلۡأَسۡبَاطِ وَمَآ أُوتِيَ مُوسَىٰ وَعِيسَىٰ وَمَآ أُوتِيَ ٱلنَّبِيُّونَ مِن رَّبِّهِمۡ لَا نُفَرِّقُ بَيۡنَ أَحَدٖ مِّنۡهُمۡ وَنَحۡنُ لَهُۥ مُسۡلِمُونَ ١٣٦ ﴾

Say (O Muslims), "We believe in Allaah and that which has been sent down to us and that which has been sent down to Ibraheem (Abraham), Ismaa'eel (Ishmael), Is'haaq (Isaac), Ya'qoob (Jacob), and to Al-Asbât, and that which has been given to Moosaa (Moses) and 'Eesaa (Jesus), and that which has been given to the Prophets from their Lord. We make no distinction between any of them, and for Him we are Muslims [182]

What is intended by his statement: قولوا (say) meaning: (Say) with your hearts and your tongues. Due to this, statement is not deemed to be the statement of the tongue only unless it has been restricted. Allaah, the Exalted, says:

﴿ يَقُولُونَ بِأَفۡوَٰهِهِم مَّا لَيۡسَ فِي قُلُوبِهِمۡۚ وَٱللَّهُ أَعۡلَمُ بِمَا يَكۡتُمُونَ ١٦٧ ﴾

---

[182] Soorah Al-Baqarah (2:136)

They say with their mouths what was not in their hearts. And Allaah has full knowledge of what they conceal. [183]

This is explicit in the fact that the statement is with the heart and the tongue. Due to this, whenever Ahlus-Sunnah say within their books that Al-Eemaan is statement, then this comprises the two affairs of statement with the tongue and statement of the heart. As for its indication of actions with the limbs entering into the title of Al-Eemaan, then it is within his statement:

"The lowest of them is to remove something harmful from the road."

This indicates that actions enter into the title of Al-Eemaan. For the removal of something harmful is an action that the person does and it is a part of Al-Eemaan and a branch from amongst its branches.

As for its indication for that which is within the heart to enter into the title of Al-Eemaan, is within his statement:

"And Al-Hayaa is a branch of Al-Eemaan."

---

[183] Soorah Aali Imran (3:167)

Al-Hayaa is an action from the actions of the heart and it enters into the title of Al-Eemaan. Therefore, fear, trust, fervent desire, dread and other than it from the actions of the heart which have been commanded, all of them enter into the title of Al-Eemaan.

The poet said:

"...according to the explicit statement of the Prophet,"

Here the term مُصَرَّحٌ (explicit) is a subject, the predicate of which has been delayed in mention, and it is a sentence fragment.

"Upon the statement of the Prophet (ﷺ)" These three affairs have been explicitly mentioned, as the poet said, within the statement of the Prophet (ﷺ) in many Ahaadeeth. So he who says this then his statement is built upon that which has come from the Messenger (ﷺ). From that which indicates explicitly the fact that these affairs enter into al-Eemaan is that Hadeeth of the delegation of Abul-Qays which is affirmed within the two Saheehs and other than them from the Hadeeth of Ibn 'Abbaas, may Allaah be pleased with him, from the prophet (ﷺ) that he said to the delegation of Abul-Qays:

آمركم بأربع الإيمان بالله وهل تدرون ما الإيمان بالله وهل تدرون ما الإيمان بالله ؟ شهادة أن لا إله إلا الله ، وإقام الصلاة ، وإيتاء الزكاة ، وصم رمضان وتعطوا من المغانم الخمس

"I command you with four: Eemaan in Allaah; and do you know what Eemaan in Allaah is? It is that you testify that none has the right to be worshipped except Allaah, establish the Salaah, pay the Zakat, fast Ramadhaan, and that you give one-fifth of the war booty."[184]

This is explicit in mentioning the fact that actions enter the title of Al-Eemaan and the texts which bear this meaning are many.

The poet said: *"...it decreases sometimes,"* meaning, that Eemaan, at times, decreases. Within this line of poetry, is affirmation from the poet that Eemaan increases and decreases, it gains strength and it is weakened. As for the increase of Eemaan it is explicitly mentioned in the Qur'aan. Allaah, the Exalted, said:

[184] Reported by Al-Bukhaaree no. 35 and Muslim no. 17.

﴿وَإِذَا مَآ أُنزِلَتۡ سُورَةٞ فَمِنۡهُم مَّن يَقُولُ أَيُّكُمۡ زَادَتۡهُ هَٰذِهِۦٓ إِيمَٰنٗاۚ فَأَمَّا
ٱلَّذِينَ ءَامَنُواْ فَزَادَتۡهُمۡ إِيمَٰنٗا وَهُمۡ يَسۡتَبۡشِرُونَ ١٢٤﴾

And whenever there comes down a Soorah (chapter from the Qur'aan), some of them (hypocrites) say: "Which of you has had his Faith increased by it?" As for those who believe, it has increased their Faith, and they rejoice. [185]

Allaah, the Exalted, also said:

﴿وَيَزِيدُ ٱللَّهُ ٱلَّذِينَ ٱهۡتَدَوۡاْ هُدٗىۗ وَٱلۡبَٰقِيَٰتُ ٱلصَّٰلِحَٰتُ خَيۡرٌ عِندَ رَبِّكَ ثَوَابٗا
وَخَيۡرٞ مَّرَدًّا ٧٦﴾

And Allaah increases in guidance those who walk aright. And the righteous good deeds that last, are better with your Lord, for reward and better for resort. [186]

And Allaah has said:

﴿وَيَخِرُّونَ لِلۡأَذۡقَانِ يَبۡكُونَ وَيَزِيدُهُمۡ خُشُوعٗا۩ ١٠٩﴾

---

[185] Soorah At-Tawbah (9:124)

[186] Soorah Maryam (19:76)

And they fall down on their faces weeping and it adds to their humility.[187]

And guidance as well as Al-Khushoo' is from Al-Eemaan.

As for its decrease, it is explicitly mentioned in the Sunnah. The Messenger of Allaah (ﷺ) said:

ما رأيت من ناقصات عقل ودين

"I have not seen anyone as deficient in their intellect and their religion..."[188]

This deficiency is not considered a defect of the woman, for she is commanded to leave off the Salaah and fasting while she is menstruating. The Prophet (ﷺ) said:

من رأى منكم منكرا فليغيره بيده ، فإن لم يستطع فبلسانه ، فإن لم يستطع فبقلبه ، وذلك أضعف الإيمان

"He from amongst you who sees an evil then let him change it with his hand; and if he is not able then let him do so with his tongue;

---

[187] Soorah Al-Isra (17:109)

[188] Reported by Al-Bukhaaree no. 304 and Muslim no. 79.

> **and if he is not able then let him do so with his heart and that is the weakest of Al-Eemaan."** [189]

There have come explicit narrations from the companions that Eemaan increases and decreases. On the authority of 'Umayr ibn Habeeb Al-Katmee; it is mentioned that he said: *"Eemaan increases and decreases."* It was said: *"And how is it increased and decreased?"* He said: *"If we remember Allaah, praise Him, and Glorify Him, then this is its increase, and if we are heedless and forgetful, then that is its decrease."* In this regard many narrations have come from them and from the companions in general. Rather, it is a point of consensus and an affair upon which there is agreement.

The poet said: *"And because of obedience it grows,"* meaning, Eemaan increases with the obedience of Allaah. It is said نَمَى يَنْمِي نَمْياً and نماءً; meaning it increased and became abundant. In some manuscripts it reads بطاعته ينمو (It grows with His obedience), and this bears the same meaning. It is said: نَمَا ينمو نُمُوًّا; meaning it increased and became abundant.

The author of Lisaan Al-'Arab said: "نَمَى *or* النِمَاءُ *means increase.* نَمَى ينمي نمياً and نماءً; *all mean to increase and*

---

[189] Reported by Muslim no. 49.

become abundant. They say ينمو نموّاً *(a growth developed)."*[190]

The poet said: *"...and on the scale it will out way other things,"* meaning, within the scale on the Day of Judgment it will be heavy due to its increasing by way of obedience and staying away from disobedience. Within these two lines of poetry, the poet clarifies two affairs regarding the 'Aqeedah of Ahlus-Sunnah as it relates to Eemaan and they are: **Firstly**, that Eemaan is statements and actions**. Secondly**, that it increases and decreases. The first contains a refutation of the Murji'ah and the second contains a refutation against Murji'ah, the Khawaarij, and the Mu'tazilah who say that Eemaan is one entity and it does not increase nor does it decrease.

That which has caused all of these groups to become corrupt in their religion is their belief that Eemaan is all one entity and it is not in parts; therefore if some of it goes then it departs in totality. Moreover, Eemaan increases by way of a number of affairs which it is befitting that the Muslim be diligent upon in order that he may increase his Eemaan. From them there is reflecting upon the Qur'aan as well as knowing the Names and Attributes of Allaah and pondering over the

[190] Lisaan Al-'Arab by ibn Mandhoor 8/4551.

verses of Allaah and His creation, as well as studying the Seerah of the Messenger (ﷺ) and the Seerah of the elite from amongst the believers and exerting efforts in doing acts of obedience.

It decreases by way of a number affairs which it is befitting that the Muslim beware of in order that he may safeguard his Eemaan from them. From them is following the footsteps of Shaytaan, obeying one's soul which calls him to evil, as well as being put to trial by the Dunyaa and mixing with the people of evil and corruption, as well as heedlessness, turning away, and following desires. The Muslim who has intellect sincerely advises himself as it relates to his Eemaan in order that his scales may be made heavy on the day that he meets Allaah, the Mighty and Majestic. Allaah says:

﴿وَالْوَزْنُ يَوْمَئِذٍ الْحَقُّ ۚ فَمَن ثَقُلَتْ مَوَازِينُهُ فَأُولَٰئِكَ هُمُ الْمُفْلِحُونَ ﴿٨﴾﴾

So as for those whose scale (of good deeds) will be heavy, they will be the successful (by entering Paradise). [191]

[191] Soorah Al-A'raf (7:8)

The poet, may Allaah have mercy upon him, indicates this meaning when he said:

> *"and on the scale it will outweigh other things."*

WARNING AGAINST FOLLOWING OPINIONS AND THE ONE WHO CRITICIZES THE HADEETH AND ITS PEOPLE

(31) وَدَعْ عنكَ آراءَ الرِّجالِ وَقولَهُم فَقَوْلُ رَسُولِ اللهِ أَزكى وَأَشْرَحُ

(32) وَلا تَكُ مِن قَوْمٍ تَلَهَّوْ بِدِينِهِم فَتَطْعنَ في أَهلِ الحَدَيثِ وتَقْدَحُ

31. And abandon the opinions of people and their statements,

Since the statement of the Messenger of Allaah is purer and comforting to the chest.

32. And do not be from those who play games with their religion,

Attacking the people of Hadeeth and reviling them.

Explanation

The poet said: *"And abandon,"* meaning, leave off beware of and avoid: *"...the opinions or men and their statements,"* Meaning, do not build your religion and your creed upon generic ideas and newly invented statements. Rather, build it upon the Book and the Sunnah; for in the two of them lies safety and security.

Many statements have come from the Salaf, may Allaah have mercy upon them, warning against opinions and criticizing opinion and its people. From that is the statement of 'Umar, may Allaah be pleased with him, that he said:

> **"Beware of the people of opinions, for indeed they are the enemies of the religion; they have become tired of the Sunnah and memorizing it, and thus began to act upon their intellects."**[192]

'Alee, may Allaah be pleased with him, said:

> **"If the religion were based upon opinion, then wiping the bottom of the Khuff will take more precedence then wiping its top part."**[193]

What is intended by opinion here is the blameworthy opinion which is based upon guessing, speculation, and mere intellect, along with negation of the texts and

---

192 Reported by Ad-Daaraqutnee within As-Sunan narration no. 12

193 Reported by Aboo Daawud no. 162 Al-Albaanee graded it Saheeh within Saheeh Sunan Abee Daawud no. 162.

neglecting them, hindering the people from them and turning away from them. This is the opinion which causes innovations to spring forth, and brings about misguidance and by way of it the Names and Attributes of Allaah are negated. Therefore, the likes of these negative opinions and false assumptions should not be paid attention to by the Muslim. Rather, it is obligatory that they be rejected and that one beware of them and not be deceived by the beautification of them by the people of falsehood. Al-'Awzaa'ee, may Allaah have mercy upon him, said:

> "Cling to the narrations even if the people reject you, and beware or the opinions of men even if they beautify them for you by way of their speech, for indeed the affair is made clear and you are upon the straight way."

The poet said: *"...the opinions of men,"* the mention of men here has no import; for false opinions are blameworthy whether they are from men or women. However, he mentioned men here because in most cases they are the people of opinions.

The poet said: *"...the statement of the Messenger of Allaah* (صَلَّى اللهُ عَلَيْهِ وَسَلَّمَ)*,"* meaning, the statement which is sound and affirmed from him (صَلَّى اللهُ عَلَيْهِ وَسَلَّمَ). He said: "...is purer," meaning, it is more pure, more wholesome and more sincere. In some of the manuscripts it reads: "أولى (takes more precedence)" meaning, it takes precedence in being accepted and given preference.

The poet said: *"...and comforting to the chest,"* meaning, it is comforting to the chests and the hearts and brings about more tranquility. The people on the Day of Judgment will not be asked except regarding that, as Allaah, the Exalted, said:

﴿ وَيَوْمَ يُنَادِيهِمْ فَيَقُولُ مَاذَآ أَجَبْتُمُ ٱلْمُرْسَلِينَ ﴿٦٥﴾ ﴾

And (remember) the Day (Allaah) will call to them, and say: "What answer gave you to the Messengers?" [194]

So they will not be asked about the opinions of men and their statements, rather they will be asked regarding that which the messengers came to them with, upon them be prayers and peace.

The poet said:

"...and do not be from those who play games with their religion, attacking the people of Hadeeth and reviling them,"

---

194 Soorah Al-Qasas (28:65)

This line of poetry is extremely appropriate for that which came before it since the poet, in the first line, mentioned generally the Sunnah and the transmissions from the companions and Taabi'oon and those after them; for these are the best of the people and the most noble of them, yet they did not have with them theological opinions nor intellectual philosophies, or generic statements. That which they had with them was simply clinging to the text and holding fast to the prophetic Sunnah. Then this line of poetry warns against the path of the people of folly and falsehood who revile these Imaams and eminent scholars.

He said: *"...and do not be..."* meaning, beware of being, O person of the Sunnah; O he who Allaah has guided to clinging to the guidance of the best of this Ummah: *"...from those who play games with their religion,"* meaning, from those who take their religion as pastime and play. This comprises the people of innovations and desires as well as the people of sins and wickedness. Indeed all of them have a share in that; be it small or large due to their ignorance of the Sunnah. He who is ignorant of a thing will take it as his enemy.

The poet said: *"...attacking the people of Hadeeth and reviling them,"* this is the result of taking ones religion as pastime and play; belittlement of the people of truth and accusing those who cling to the Sunnah as well revilement of the people of goodness virtue and nobility. This is the plot of the bankrupt people in every time and place.

Allaah, the Exalted: says:

﴿ إِنَّ ٱلَّذِينَ أَجْرَمُوا۟ كَانُوا۟ مِنَ ٱلَّذِينَ ءَامَنُوا۟ يَضْحَكُونَ ﴿٢٩﴾ وَإِذَا مَرُّوا۟ بِهِمْ يَتَغَامَزُونَ ﴿٣٠﴾ وَإِذَا ٱنقَلَبُوٓا۟ إِلَىٰٓ أَهْلِهِمُ ٱنقَلَبُوا۟ فَكِهِينَ ﴿٣١﴾ ﴾

Verily! (During the worldly life) those who committed crimes used to laugh at those who believed. And whenever they passed by them, used to wink one to another (in mockery); And when they returned to their own people, they would return jesting; [195]

If the people were a people of truth and evidence, then they would have opposed it with proof and they would have combated evidence with evidence and proof with proof. However, there is no strategy for the bankrupt negator except criticism, revilement, and mockery.

From the signs of the people of desires and innovations is revilement of the people of Hadeeth and narrations,

[195] Soorah Al-Mutaffifin (83:29-31)

and this is from the greatest iniquities and the most severe evils. Hence, the people of Hadeeth do not bring anything except clarity, beautiful manners and good treatment. Some of the people of knowledge have said in clarification of the virtue of the people of Hadeeth and clarification of some of their virtues and excellence:

> "Allaah has rewarded the people of Hadeeth with a great reward and has placed them for eternity on the highest level, were it not for the concern which they gave to the Hadeeth and their memorizing it and their negating from it all aspects of falsehood and their spending their lives seeking it and researching it with seriousness, then the Faqeeh would not have known the authentic Hadeeth from that which is repugnant and falsehood. And that which has been mentioned in general will not be made clear from that which is specific and one will not know that which is obligatory in general from that which is supererogatory. They exerted therein great efforts and have spent a large portion of their lives devoted to it. Therefore, loving them is obligatory upon every Muslim and none hates them other than one who is ignorant."

We ask Allaah to reward them on our behalf and on behalf of the Muslims with the best reward, and to raise their rank and place it amongst 'Illiyyeen, and to give them an honorable mention amongst the latter peoples and to forgive us and them all together.

CONCLUSION OF THE POEM

(33) إذا مَا اعتقـدْتَ الدَّهْرَ يا صَاحِ هذِه فَأَنْـتَ عَلـى خَيْـرٍ تَبِيتُ وتُصْبِحُ

33. If you keep the belief contained within this poem, for all of your life, O my companion,

Then you will be upon goodness, day and night

Explanation

When the poet concluded his poem having gathered therein the most important principles of the creed of Ahlus-Sunnah, he ended with this line in order to emphasize therein the importance of this creed; and the importance of preserving it. He said:

"If you keep the belief contained within this poem for all your life, O my companion you will be upon goodness day and night,"

meaning, if you, O my companion, are upon this creed which is derived from the Book of Allaah and the Sunnah and His Messenger (ﷺ), you are from its people and cling to it and you preserve it, then you will be upon good from that which remains from your life based upon this creed.

The term إذا (if) is a tool of condition and it denotes the future of that which remains from time, and the word مَا is additional.

The statement of the poet: *"...you keep the belief,"* Al-I'tiqaad is derived from *Al-'Aqd* which is a connection. This is because it is a must that one attaches his heart to the affairs of creed by way of having Eemaan in them and clinging to them without doubt and uncertainty. If there is found any doubt or uncertainty, then it is not therefore considered to be 'Aqeedah.

Allaah, the Exalted, said:

﴿إِنَّمَا ٱلْمُؤْمِنُونَ ٱلَّذِينَ ءَامَنُوا۟ بِٱللَّهِ وَرَسُولِهِۦ ثُمَّ لَمْ يَرْتَابُوا۟﴾

Only those are the believers who have believed in Allaah and His Messenger, and afterward doubt not. [196]

Meaning, they are certain and they have no doubt.

The statement of the poet: الدَّهْرَ means, for the duration of your life and the full extent of your existence. In this there is proof that the creed will not benefit the servant unless he remains upon it up until Allaah causes him to die. As Allaah, the Exalted, said:

[196] Soorah Al-Hujurat (49:15)

﴿ يَٰٓأَيُّهَا ٱلَّذِينَ ءَامَنُوا۟ ٱتَّقُوا۟ ٱللَّهَ حَقَّ تُقَاتِهِۦ وَلَا تَمُوتُنَّ إِلَّا وَأَنتُم مُّسْلِمُونَ ﴿١٠٢﴾ ﴾

O you who believe! Fear Allaah as He should be feared, and die not except in a state of Islaam. [197]

The Messenger of Allaah (ﷺ) said regarding the Du'aa for the deceased:

اللهم من أحييته منّا فأحيه على الإسلام ومن توفيته منّا فتوفه على الإيمان

> **"O Allaah, he whom You give life from amongst us then make him live upon Al-Islaam and he whom You cause to die from amongst us then make him to die upon Al-Eemaan."**[198]

The poet said: "يا صاحِ" this is an abbreviation for the word Saahib, it means: *O my companion*. This is from the subtleties of the poet, may Allaah have mercy upon him, and his excellence in love and the beautiful nature of his advice, may Allaah have mercy upon him, forgive him, and reward him with the best reward.

---

[197] Soorah Aali Imran (3:102)

[198] Reported by Aboo Daawud no. 3201. Al-Albaanee graded it Saheeh within Saheeh Sunan Abee Daawud no. 3201. Refer as well the book Ahkaam Al-Janaa'iz pg. 157.

The poet said: "هذِه ..." this is an indication to the magnificent principles which were mentioned within this poem; and they are noble principles built upon the Book and the Sunnah. He who clings to them will be safe and he who deviates from them will be destroyed.

The poet said: "فَأَنْتَ (...then you)" meaning, you will be... and this is the result of the condition being fulfilled.

He said: *"...will be upon goodness day and night,"* in another manuscript it reads: "In the evening and in the morning," meaning, as long as you stand upon these principles and cling to them, then your morning and your evening; your sleep and your wakefulness will all be in a state of goodness and upon goodness. In this is an indication to the fact that the correct creed brings about safety and goodness in all circumstances; praiseworthy endings and continuous goodness as well as an excellent fate are brought about as a result, and it calls to righteousness, acts of obedience, praiseworthy characteristics, noble etiquettes, and good deeds.

In this as well is a call to firmness upon this correct creed and a warning against shiftiness and game playing, as is the state of the people of desires. As for Ahlus-Sunnah their creed is firm and their Eemaan is solid; their certainty is continuous by the Tawfeeq of Allaah, the Mighty and Majestic,

May Allaah make us all firm upon Al-Eemaan, and may He provide us with an excellent ending.

By way of this, the poet, may Allaah have mercy upon him, ended his poem and in spite of its conciseness it is replete with principles of the creed and the foundations of Al-Eemaan. That which was not mentioned therein is indicated by way of that which was mentioned. And Allaah knows best.

May prayer and peace of Allaah be upon Muhammad, his family and his companions all together.

تم بحمد الله